EXPLANATORY NOTES

CHILDREN AND FAMILIES ACT 2014

GRAN*GIS* UK Publishing

Adapted and published by GRANGIS (Grand Register Library).
Online: www.grangis.com
E-mail: contact@grangis.com

In this version:
ISBN: 979-8-88559-035-8

Note: This is the original version (as it was originally enacted). Title, sub-title and the generated date is as marked on the pages.

EXPLANATORY NOTES

CHILDREN AND FAMILIES ACT 2014

COMMENTARY ON SECTIONS

PART 3 - CHILDREN AND YOUNG PEOPLE IN ENGLAND WITH SPECIAL EDUCATIONAL NEEDS OR DISABILITIES

Local authority functions: general principles

Section 19: Local authority functions: Supporting and involving children and young people

Special educational needs etc

Section 20: When a child or young person has special educational needs

Section 21: Special educational provision, health care provision and social care provision

Identifying children and young people with special educational needs and disabilities

Section 22: Identifying children and young people with special educational needs and disabilities

Section 23: Duty of health bodies to bring certain children to local authority's attention

Children and young people for whom a local authority is responsible

Section 24: When a local authority is responsible for a child or young person

Education, health and care provision: integration and joint commissioning

Section 25: Promoting integration

Section 26: Joint commissioning arrangements

Review of education and care provision

Section 27: Duty to keep education and care provision under review

Co-operation and assistance

Section 28: Co-operating generally: local authority functions

Section 29: Co-operating generally: governing body functions

Information and advice

Section 30: Local offer

Section 31: Co-operating in specific cases: local authority functions

Section 32: Advice and information

Mainstream education

Section 33: Children and young people with EHC plans

Section 34: Children and young people with special educational needs but no EHC plan

Assessment

Education, health and care plans

Appeals, mediation and dispute resolution

Supplementary

PART 4 – CHILDCARE ETC

PART 5 – WELFARE OF CHILDREN

Section 75E: Entitlement to shared parental leave: birth

Section 75F: Entitlement to leave under section 75E: further provision

Section 75G: Entitlement to shared parental leave: adoption

Section 75H: Entitlement to leave under section 75G: further provision

Section 75I: Rights during and after shared parental leave

Section 75J: Redundancy and dismissal

Section 75K: Chapter 1B: supplemental

Section 118: Exclusion or curtailment of other statutory rights to leave

Statutory shared parental pay

Section 119: Statutory shared parental pay

Section 171ZU: Entitlement: birth

Section 171ZV: Entitlement: adoption

Section 171ZW: Entitlement: general

Section 171ZX: Liability to make payments

Section 171ZY: Rate and period of pay

Section 171ZZ: Restrictions on contracting out

Section 171ZZ1: Relationship with contractual remuneration

Section 171ZZ2: Crown employment

Section 171ZZ3: Special classes of person

Section 171ZZ4: Part 12ZC: supplementary

Section 171ZZ5: Power to apply Part 12ZC

Section 120: Curtailment of statutory pay periods and exclusion of statutory pay

Other statutory rights

Section 121: Statutory rights to leave and pay of prospective adopters with whom looked after children are placed

Section 122: Statutory rights to leave and pay of applicants for parental orders

Section 123: Statutory paternity pay: notice requirement and period of payment

HANSARD REFERENCES

These notes refer to the Children and Families Act 2014 (c.6) which received Royal Assent on 13 March 2014

CHILDREN AND FAMILIES ACT 2014

EXPLANATORY NOTES

INTRODUCTION

1. These explanatory notes relate to the Children and Families Act 2014 which received Royal Assent on 13 March 2014. They have been prepared by the Department for Education, the Ministry of Justice and the Department for Business, Innovation and Skills in conjunction with the Department for Work and Pensions and the Department of Health. Their purpose is to assist the reader in understanding the Act. They do not form part of the Act and have not been endorsed by Parliament.

2. The notes need to be read in conjunction with the Act. They are not, and are not meant to be, a comprehensive description of the Act. So where a section or part of a section does not seem to require any explanation or comment, none is given.

BACKGROUND AND SUMMARY

3. The Act takes forward a range of Government commitments which are intended to improve services for key groups of vulnerable children (children in the adoption and care systems, those affected by decisions of the family courts and those with special educational needs and disabilities) and to support families in balancing home and work life, particularly when children are very young. It takes forward legislation that has been announced in a range of Government documents over the past 2 years, including:

   - An Action Plan for Adoption: Tackling Delay (March 2012).
   - Further Action on Adoption: Finding More Loving Homes (January 2013).
   - The Government Response to the Family Justice Review (February 2012).
   - Support and aspiration: A new approach to special educational needs and disability: Progress and next steps (May 2012).
   - More great childcare (January 2013) and More affordable childcare (July 2013).
   - The Government Response to the Modern Workplaces consultation (November 2012).

4. The Act contains provisions on a range of policies which span the responsibilities of the Department for Education, the Ministry of Justice, the Department for Business, Innovation and Skills, the Department for Work and Pensions and the Department of Health. It contains measures intended to remove barriers to adoption; reform the family justice system and the special educational needs system and ensure that services place children and young people at the centre of decision making and support. It contains measures which relate to the welfare of children, including areas such as: child performance; protecting children and young people from tobacco and nicotine addiction; young carers and parent carers; "staying put" arrangements; supporting pupils at school with medical conditions; reform of children's homes; clarifying the Secretary of State's intervention powers; and free school lunches. The Act contains measures which support wider changes to childcare; introduces a new system of shared

parental leave following childbirth or adoption; and extends to all employees the right to request flexible working. Through its reforms to the functions and role of the Children's Commissioner, the Act is intended to ensure that children in England have a strong advocate for their rights.

5. Pre-legislative scrutiny was conducted in relation to Parts 1, 2, 3 and 6 during 2012. The Government published its response in the Command paper *Children and Families Bill: Contextual Information and Responses to Pre-Legislative Scrutiny* (CM8540) on 5 February 2013.

6. The Act consists of 10 Parts, 140 sections and 7 Schedules.

7. Where explanatory notes are provided for Schedules, these are included in the notes for the relevant sections. Annex A of this document sets out further detail relating to the parental involvement provision.

Part 1: Adoption and contact

8. Part 1 of the Act contains provisions to give effect to proposals in *An Action Plan for Adoption: Tackling Delay,* published by the Department for Education on 14 March 2012, and *Further Action on Adoption: Finding More Loving Homes*, published on 24 January 2013. These set out proposals to speed up the adoption process and enable more children to be placed in stable, loving homes with less delay and disruption. The Act includes provisions which are intended to:

- Allow persons with a prescribed relationship to a person adopted before 30 December 2005 to have access to intermediary services to facilitate contact between them and the adopted person's birth relatives;
- Encourage local authorities to place children for whom they are considering adoption with their potential permanent carers more swiftly, by requiring a local authority looking after a child for whom they are considering adoption to place them with foster carers who are also approved prospective adopters, on a fostering basis. The provisions require the local authority first to consider family and friend carers;
- Reduce delay by removing the explicit legal wording around a child's ethnicity so that black and minority ethnic children are not left waiting in care longer than necessary because local authorities are seeking a perfect or partial ethnic match;
- Enable the Secretary of State to require local authorities to commission adopter recruitment services from one or more other adoption agencies;
- Give approved prospective adopters a more active role in identifying possible matches with children for whom the local authority are considering adoption, or children whom the local authority are satisfied ought to be placed for adoption but whom they are not yet authorised to place by virtue of parental consent or a placement order, by amending the current restrictions in relation to "public inspection or search" of the Adoption and Children Act Register so that they can access the register directly, subject to appropriate safeguards;
- Improve the current provision of adoption support by placing new duties on local authorities to provide personal budgets upon request and to give prospective adopters and adoptive parents information about their entitlements to support;
- Make changes to the arrangements for contact between children in care and their birth parents, guardians and certain others and adopted children and their birth families, former guardians and certain others with the aim of reducing the disruption that inappropriate contact can cause to adoptive placements.

9. Pre-legislative scrutiny of the provisions on "Fostering for Adoption" and ethnicity was undertaken by the House of Lords Select Committee on Adoption Legislation. The Committee's *Interim Report* containing its recommendations on these provisions

was published on 19 December 2012. The Government response was published on 5 February 2013 as part of *Children and Families Bill 2013: Contextual Information and Responses to Pre-Legislative Scrutiny.*

Part 2: Family justice

10. Part 2 makes changes to improve the operation of the family justice system, as recommended by the independent Family Justice Review and accepted by the Government in its response published on 6 February 2012. The Family Justice Review, chaired by David Norgrove, was set up by the Government in 2010 to look at the family justice system and make recommendations as to how the system could be changed for the benefit of children and families. An *Interim Report* was published in March 2011 and the Family Justice Review Final Report was published in November 2011.

11. In respect of private family law (by which is meant the law about resolving disputes between family members, as distinct from public family law, about intervention by public authorities), the Act includes provisions to:

- Require a potential applicant to attend a family mediation, information and assessment meeting to find out about and consider mediation before being able to apply for certain types of court order;
- Send a clear signal to separated parents that courts will take account of the principle that both should continue to be involved in their children's lives where that is safe and consistent with the child's welfare, which remains the court's paramount consideration;
- Introduce a "child arrangements order", replacing residence and contact orders;
- Make changes so that when a child arrangements order is breached, the court can direct the parties to undertake activities designed to help them understand the importance of complying with the order and making it work;
- Streamline court processes in proceedings for a decree of divorce, nullity of marriage, or judicial separation (or, in relation to a civil partnership, for a dissolution, nullity or separation order) by removing the requirement for the court to consider whether it should exercise any of its powers under the Children Act 1989. Arrangements for children can be decided at any time through separate proceedings under the Children Act 1989.

12. In respect of public family law, the Act includes provisions to:

- Introduce a maximum 26 week time limit for completing care and supervision proceedings with the possibility of extending the time limit in a particular case for up to eight weeks at a time, should that be necessary to resolve the proceedings justly;
- Ensure that the timetable for the case is child focused and decisions about it are made with explicit reference to the child's welfare;
- Make it explicit that, when the court considers a care plan, it should focus on those issues essential to deciding whether to make a care order; and
- Remove the eight week time limit on the duration of initial interim care orders and interim supervision orders, and the four week time limit on subsequent orders, and allow the court to make interim orders for the length of time it sees fit, although not extending beyond the date when the relevant care or supervision order proceedings are disposed of.

13. In respect of experts, the Act includes provision to ensure that expert evidence in children proceedings is permitted only when necessary to resolve the case justly, taking account of factors including the impact on the welfare of the child, and

whether the information could be obtained from one of the parties already involved in the proceedings. Family Procedure Rules are to prescribe the meaning of "children proceedings" which may include both private and public law proceedings.

14. Pre-legislative scrutiny of the family justice sections was undertaken by the House of Commons Justice Select Committee. The Committee published its report on 14 December 2012 and the provisions in Part 2 reflect the Government's response to the report, published on 5 February 2013 (*Children and Families Bill 2013: Contextual Information and Responses to Pre-Legislative Scrutiny)*.

Part 3: Children and young people in England with special educational needs or disabilities

15. Part 3 of the Act contains provisions following the Green Paper *Support and Aspiration: A new approach to special educational needs and disability* published by the Department for Education on 18 March 2011 and the follow up *Progress and Next Steps* published 15 May 2012.

16. The provisions are a major reform of the present statutory framework for identifying children and young people with special educational needs (SEN), assessing their needs and making provision for them. They require local authorities to keep local provision for children and young people with SEN and disabilities under review, to co-operate with their partners to plan and commission provision for those children and young people and publish clear information on services they expect to be available. The provisions set out the statutory framework for identifying, and assessing the needs of, children and young people with SEN who require support beyond that which is normally available. Statements made under section 324 of the Education Act 1996 and Learning Difficulty Assessments made under section 139A of the Learning and Skills Act 2000 are replaced by new 0-25 Education, Health and Care plans (EHC plans) for both children and young people. The provisions place a new requirement on health commissioners to deliver the health care services specified in plans.

17. The provisions extend the rights that parents of children with statements of SEN currently have, to express a preference for the school they wish their child to attend, to young people in education and training (including further education). In addition, they widen the institutions for which they can express a preference to include Academy schools, further education colleges and sixth form colleges, non-maintained special schools and independent special schools and independent specialist colleges approved for this purpose by the Secretary of State.

18. The provisions are also intended to give parents and young people greater control over the way their support is provided through involvement with local authorities in reviewing services and through the option of personal budgets in certain circumstances. They introduce a requirement to consider mediation before appeals are made to the First-tier Tribunal. This is to help resolve disagreements without the need for Tribunal appeals wherever possible. The provisions also extend the right to appeal to young people in education and training (including further education); include a power to pilot giving children the right to make appeals to the Tribunal themselves, rather than it having to be through their parent; and to pilot the Tribunal making recommendations on the health and social care provision set out in an EHC plan.

19. The sections replace and extend, in relation to England, provisions in Part 4 of the Education Act 1996, associated regulations, and sections 139A to 139C of the Learning and Skills Act 2000, which will be repealed in relation to children and young people in the area of a local authority in England. Regulations will set out the detailed requirements of particular provisions where provided for in the sections. A statutory Code of Practice will be developed to provide guidance on the new framework for SEN, for the approval of Parliament.

20. Pre-legislative scrutiny of the SEN provisions was undertaken by the House of Commons Education Select Committee. The Committee published its report on 18 December 2012 and the provisions in Part 3 reflect the Government's response to the report, published on 5 February 2013 (*Children and Families Bill 2013: Contextual Information and Responses to Pre-Legislative Scrutiny*).

Part 4: Childcare etc

21. Part 4 of the Act contains various provisions relating to childcare, some of which flow from proposals described in *More Great Childcare* which the Government published on 29 January 2013 and which includes the Government's response to Professor Cathy Nutbrown's report, *Foundations for Quality* (published in June 2012). Section 3D of *More Great Childcare* refers to the plans to introduce childminder agencies.

22. This Part contains provision:

- For childminder agencies (that is persons who are registered in the appropriate childcare register by Her Majesty's Chief Inspector of Education, Children's Services and Skills ("the Chief Inspector") and who are therefore able to register childminders and other providers of childcare on domestic premises for the purposes of Part 3 of the Childcare Act 2006);
- For the Chief Inspector to charge a fee for carrying out an inspection of early years childcare provision where the inspection is carried out at the request of the provider and the Chief Inspector is required by the Secretary of State to conduct the inspection;
- To allow regulations to be made about the way local authorities meet their duty to secure early years provision for young children;
- Repealing the duty in section 11 of the Childcare Act 2006 on English local authorities to prepare, at least every three years, an assessment of the sufficiency of the provision of childcare in their area;
- To remove the requirements in section 28 of the Education Act 2002 on governing bodies of maintained schools to consult with local authorities, staff and parents on whether to offer community facilities or services. This would remove a current burden on schools considering offering before and after school childcare, amongst other services. It also removes the requirement for the governing bodies to have regard to advice or guidance from the Secretary of State or local authorities before providing such facilities;
- For Her Majesty's Revenue and Customs (HMRC) to undertake preparatory expenditure in relation to the introduction of a scheme for providing assistance in respect of the costs of childcare.

Part 5: Welfare of Children

23. Part 5 of the Act contains various provisions relating to the welfare of children, including to:

- Repeal section 38 of the Children and Young Persons Act 1963, in relation to England and Wales, removing restrictions on the circumstances in which a local authority can issue a performance licence to a child under the age of 14;
- Protect children and young people from tobacco and nicotine addiction;
- Consolidate legislation relating to the rights and support for young carers and parent carers, and extend their rights to assessment;
- Enable former looked after children to continue to live ("stay put") with their former foster parents until age 21, if the local authority determines that it would be

appropriate for them to do so and both the young person and the foster parent wish to make a "staying put" arrangement;

- Amend section 22 of the Children Act 1989 to require local authorities in England to appoint an officer for the purpose of discharging the authority's duty to promote the educational achievement of the children they look after;
- Place a duty on governing bodies of maintained schools, proprietors of Academies and management committees of pupil referral units to make arrangements for supporting pupils at school with medical conditions;
- Clarify the law in relation to the Secretary of State's power to intervene under section 497A(4A) of the Education Act 1996 and section 50 of the Children Act 2004, where a local authority is failing to deliver children's services to an adequate standard;
- Support the reform of children's homes, particularly by enabling the development of a regulation and inspection framework that sets high standards for children in residential care and offers them the support required to achieve positive outcomes;
- Ensure that all state-funded schools – both maintained schools and Academies – have an obligation to provide free school lunches on request for all pupils in reception, year one and year two.

Part 6: The Children's Commissioner

24. Part 6 of the Act implements the recommendations from John Dunford's independent review of the Children's Commissioner (*Review of the Office of the Children's Commissioner (England): December 2010*), which concluded that there were strong arguments for retaining the office of Children's Commissioner ("OCC"), but that the legislative framework had prevented the Commissioner from having sufficient impact on children's lives. The provisions in the Act aim to remove the barriers that John Dunford identified, in particular by:

- Amending the Commissioner's primary function to one of promoting and protecting children's rights;
- Making the Commissioner more clearly independent from Government;
- Providing for greater scrutiny of the Commissioner's impact, through an annual report to Parliament;
- Combining the functions of the Commissioner with the activities currently carried out by the Children's Rights Director;
- Clarifying the Commissioner's powers and remit.

25. Pre-legislative scrutiny of the OCC sections was undertaken by the Joint Committee on Human Rights (JCHR). The Government's response to the report was published on 5 February 2013 (*Children and Families Bill 2013: Contextual Information and Responses to Pre-Legislative Scrutiny*).

Part 7: Statutory rights to leave and pay

26. Part 7 of the Act delivers the legislative commitments made in the Government Response to the Modern Workplaces consultation (November 2012). The provisions create a new employment right to shared parental leave and statutory shared parental pay for eligible working parents. Women continue to be eligible for maternity leave and statutory maternity pay or allowance in the same way as previously. If they choose to bring their leave and pay or allowance to an early end, eligible working parents can share up to the balance of the remaining leave and pay as shared parental leave and pay. Eligible adopters can use the new system for shared parental leave and pay. Adoption

leave and pay include prospective parents in the "Fostering for Adoption" system, and parents in a surrogacy arrangement who are eligible, and intend to apply, for a parental order.

Part 8: Time off work: Ante-natal care etc

27. Part 8 creates a new right for employees and qualifying agency workers to take unpaid time off work to attend up to two ante-natal appointments with a pregnant woman. The right is available to the pregnant woman's husband, civil partner or partner, the father or parent of the pregnant woman's child, and intended parents in a surrogacy situation who meet specified conditions.

28. Provision is made for paid and unpaid time off work for adopters to attend meetings in advance of a child being placed with them for adoption.

Part 9: Right to request flexible working

29. Part 9 provides for the expansion of the right to request flexible working from employees who are parents or carers to all employees, and the removal of the statutory process that employers must currently follow when considering requests for flexible working. The Government's policy reforms for the right to request flexible working are set out in its paper *Modern Workplaces – Government Response on Flexible Working* (published in November 2012). This Part sets out the statutory provisions to support those reforms.

30. Changes enable employers to consider requests using their existing HR processes instead of having to follow a statutory procedure.

31. These sections amend the Employment Rights Act 1996 ("ERA"). Following consultation the Advisory, Conciliation and Arbitration Service ("ACAS") has published a draft Code of Practice on handling requests to work flexibly in a reasonable manner. This Code will explain what the minimum requirements are in order to consider a request in a reasonable manner. If neither House of Parliament resolves that no further proceedings shall be taken, the Code of Practice will be issued using powers in the Trade Union and Labour Relations (Consolidation) Act 1992 and will be brought into force by order on a date appointed by the Secretary of State.

TERRITORIAL EXTENT AND APPLICATION

32. Except where stated otherwise below, the Children and Families Act 2014 extends to England and Wales only, and applies to England only. The significant exceptions are explained in the text below. Annex B sets out the territorial extent and application of each of the sections in a table.

Scotland

33. Section 7 and Schedule 1 amend sections 125 to 131 (which have not been commenced) of the Adoption and Children Act 2002, which provide for the establishment of the Adoption and Children Act Register ("the register"). The register contains information about children who are suitable for adoption and for whom the local authority are considering adoption and prospective adopters who are suitable to adopt a child. This section removes Wales and Scotland from the scope of these sections and provides for the establishment of a register that applies in relation to England only.

34. Section 94 gives the Secretary of State the power to make regulations to standardise tobacco packaging if he or she considers that they may contribute to reducing the risk of harm to or promoting the health or welfare of children. The Secretary of State must obtain the consent of the Scottish Ministers before making regulations containing provisions which would be within the legislative competence of that Parliament.

35. Part 6 of the Act (sections 107 to 116) amends Part 1 of the Children Act 2004, to reform the office of Children's Commissioner. Part 1 of that Act extends to the whole of the UK. The changes made by Part 6 apply to the Commissioner's role in promoting and protecting the rights of children in Scotland, but only in relation to non-devolved matters.

36. Parts 7, 8 and 9 of the Act (sections 117 to 134) contain amendments to the Employment Rights Act 1996 (ERA) and the Social Security Contributions and Benefits Act 1992 (SSCBA) to make provision for statutory rights to leave and pay, time off work for ante-natal and adoption appointments, and flexible working. The sections relate to reserved matters and extend to Scotland.

Northern Ireland

37. Section 94 gives the Secretary of State the power to regulate tobacco packaging if he or she considers that regulations may contribute to reducing the risk of harm to or promoting the health or welfare of children. The Secretary of State must obtain the consent of the Office of the First Minister and deputy First Minister before making regulations containing provisions which would be within the legislative competence of the Assembly.

38. Part 6 of the Act (sections 107 to 116) reform the office of Children's Commissioner. These changes apply to the Commissioner's role in promoting and protecting the rights of children in Northern Ireland, but only in relation to non-devolved matters. In some cases section 126(3) and (4), in Part 7 of the Act, also extends to Northern Ireland.

Wales

Part 1: Adoption and contact

39. Section 1 amends section 98(1) of the Adoption and Children Act 2002 so that regulations can make provision to facilitate contact between persons with a prescribed relationship to a person adopted before 30 December 2005 and the adopted person's birth relatives. Regulations will be made by the Welsh Ministers in relation to Wales.

40. In relation to section 7 and Schedule 1 see paragraphs 70 to79.

41. Sections 8 and 9 of the Act amend provisions in the Children Act 1989 and the Adoption and Children Act 2002 which deal with contact between a child in the care of the local authority and their birth family and certain other people. Family proceedings are non-devolved matters and so the provisions relating to these apply to Wales. Adoption policy and functions of local authorities in relation to adoption are matters devolved to the Welsh Government and the provisions which relate to local authorities' duties in relation to contact in the Children Act 1989 (other than section 7(2)) do not apply to Wales.

Part 2: Family justice

42. Part 2 of the Act (sections 10 to 18) makes provisions that reform the family justice system. All of the sections relate to family law and proceedings with one exception set out in the text below. Family law and proceedings are a non-devolved matter and so these provisions also apply to Wales.

43. Section 15 amends section 31A of the Children Act 1989 which relates to care orders and care planning. Care planning is an area where the National Assembly for Wales has legislative competence. The amendments to section 31A(1) confer a new power on Welsh Ministers to allow them to prescribe by regulations the time within which a care plan (which a local authority in Wales is responsible for preparing) must be prepared by the local authority.

44. In addition, section 12 introduces a "child arrangements order" which has a consequential impact on the power of Welsh Ministers to make regulations. The power that is affected is not one that falls within an area of Assembly legislative competence but the changes affect an area of Welsh Ministers' executive competence.

Part 3: Children and young people in England with special educational needs or disabilities

45. Part 3 of the Act (sections 19 to 83) makes provision that reforms the special educational needs system. These provisions extend to England and Wales, but the majority only apply in England. Schedule 3 makes consequential amendments to existing provisions so that they apply to Wales only. There will be some cross border effects, where a child or young person in England attends a school or institution in Wales, and the amendment made by section 60 applies in Wales. The amendment does not change the effect of the amended provision as it applies in Wales. Section 70 provides the Secretary of State with a power to make regulations to apply provisions in relation to those in custody, with or without modification. The Secretary of State is required to consult the Welsh Ministers before making any such regulations where they apply to a person who is detained in Wales.

Part 5: Welfare of children

46. Section 90 repeals section 38 of the Children and Young Persons Act 1963 in relation to England and Wales only, to remove restrictions on the circumstances in which a local authority can issue a performance licence to a child under the age of 14.

47. Sections 91 to 95 make provision to protect children and young people from tobacco and nicotine addiction. Section 91 introduces an offence of "proxy purchasing" of tobacco products and cigarette papers. Sections 92 and 93 provide the Secretary of State with the power to make regulations to prohibit the sale of nicotine products to persons under the age of 18. Section 94 gives the Secretary of State the power to regulate tobacco packaging if he or she considers that regulations may contribute to reducing the risk of harm to or promoting the health or welfare of children. The Secretary of State must obtain the consent of Welsh Ministers before making regulations containing provision which would be within the legislative competence of the National Assembly for Wales. Section 95 amends smoke-free legislation to provide the Secretary of State, or the Welsh Ministers in relation to Wales, with the power to make regulations to provide for a private vehicle to be smoke-free when a person under the age of 18 is present.

48. Section 101 applies to England and Wales.

Part 6: The Children's Commissioner

49. Part 6 of the Act (sections 107 to 116) reforms the office of Children's Commissioner. These changes apply to the Commissioner's role in promoting and protecting the rights of children in Wales, but only in relation to non-devolved matters.

Parts 7, 8 & 9: Statutory rights to leave and pay, Time off work: ante-natal care etc and Right to request flexible working

50. Parts 7, 8 and 9 of the Act (sections 117 to 134) make provision for statutory rights to leave and pay, time off work for ante-natal and adoption appointments, and flexible working. The sections relate to non-devolved matters and so apply to Wales.

COMMENTARY ON SECTIONS

Part 1: ADOPTION AND CONTACT

Adoption

Section 1: Contact between prescribed persons and adopted person's relatives

51. This section amends section 98(1) of the Adoption and Children Act 2002 ("the 2002 Act"). Section 98(1) of the 2002 Act allows regulations to be made to facilitate contact between persons adopted before 30 December 2005 (when the 2002 Act came into force) and their birth relatives, Section 1 extends this regulation making power so that regulations can also make provision to facilitate contact between persons with a prescribed relationship to a person adopted before 30 December 2005 and the adopted person's birth relatives.

52. Persons prescribed under these regulations will include the direct line of descendants of the adopted person (i.e. children, grandchildren) but the Department for Education intends to consult on whether it is appropriate for others, such as spouses and siblings of descendants, to be able to access the same services.

Section 2: Placement of looked after children with prospective adopters

53. This section amends section 22C of the Children Act 1989 as it applies in relation to England. New *subsection (9A)* imposes a duty on a local authority looking after a child, when they are considering adoption for the child, or are satisfied that the child ought to be placed for adoption but are not authorised to place that child for adoption, to consider placing the child in a "Fostering for Adoption" placement.

54. A "Fostering for Adoption" placement is a foster placement with foster parents who are also approved prospective adopters, in circumstances where the local authority are considering adoption as an option for the child's long term care (whether it is the only option they are considering, or one of several) or are satisfied that the child ought to be placed for adoption but do not yet have authorisation to place the child for adoption. In these circumstances the local authority will be under a duty to consider a "Fostering for Adoption" placement. Section 22C(5) of the Act will apply, and requires the local authority to place the child in "the most appropriate placement available", and section 22 of the Act will apply in relation to the decision about which placement is most appropriate, and will require the authority to act in the child's best interests. The local authority must first have considered placing the child with relatives, friends or other connected persons and have ruled them out as not being the most appropriate potential carers for the child.

Section 3: Repeal of requirement to give due consideration to ethnicity: England

55. This section amends section 1 of the 2002 Act so that *subsection (5)* does not apply in relation to local authorities in, and registered adoption societies whose principal office is in, England. Section 1(5) of that Act requires adoption agencies to give due consideration to a child's religious persuasion, racial origin and cultural and linguistic background when placing him or her for adoption.

56. Adoption agencies are required by section 1(2) and (4) of that Act to make a child's welfare throughout his or her life their paramount consideration, and to have regard to a range of matters, including the child's needs, wishes and feelings, and his or her background and other relevant characteristics, in reaching a placement decision. These provisions, therefore, mean that the adoption agency is already and will remain under a duty to have regard to the child's religious persuasion, racial origin and cultural and linguistic background, amongst other factors, where relevant. An adoption agency is also required by section 1(3) of that Act to bear in mind that any delay in coming to a decision is likely to prejudice the child's welfare.

57. The amendment to *subsection (5)* is intended to avoid any suggestion that the current legislation places a child's religious persuasion, racial origin and cultural and linguistic background above the factors in section 1(2) to (4).

Section 4: Recruitment, assessment and approval of prospective adopters

58. This section inserts a new section 3A into the 2002 Act. Section 3 of that Act requires each local authority to maintain within their area an adoption service designed to meet the needs, in relation to adoption, of, and provide facilities for: children who may be adopted; their parents and guardians; persons wishing to adopt a child; and adopted persons, their parents, natural parents and former guardians. Local authorities may provide those facilities by securing their provision by other local authorities and registered adoption societies (defined in section 2(2) of the 2002 Act). Only local authorities and registered adoption societies may make arrangements for adoption (sections 92 and 94 of the 2002 Act).

59. The new section 3A provides a new power for the Secretary of State to direct one or more named local authorities in England, or one or more descriptions of local authority in England, to make arrangements for all or any of their functions in relation to the recruitment of persons as prospective adopters; the assessment of prospective adopters' suitability to adopt a child; and the approval of prospective adopters as suitable to adopt a child, to be carried out on their behalf by one or more other adoption agencies (other local authorities or voluntary adoption agencies).

60. The new section 3A also provides a new power for the Secretary of State to require, by order, all local authorities in England to make arrangements for all or any of their functions in relation to the recruitment of persons as prospective adopters; the assessment of prospective adopters' suitability to adopt a child; and the approval of prospective adopters as suitable to adopt a child, to be carried out on their behalf by one or more other adoption agencies (other local authorities or voluntary adoption agencies). Such an order is subject to the affirmative resolution procedure and cannot be made before 1 March 2015.

Section 5: Adoption support services: personal budgets

61. This section inserts a new section 4A into the 2002 Act to make provision enabling local authorities to prepare personal budgets for adoption support services. A personal budget is an amount to be made available to secure particular adoption support services and provides a way of involving an adopted person or the parent of an adopted person ("the recipient") in securing those services.

62. Personal budgets may take the form of direct payments, where families can purchase the services themselves, notional personal budgets, which families can prepare with the local authority and which the local authority can spend on their behalf at their direction, or a combination of both.

63. Section 4A(2) requires local authorities to prepare a personal budget with respect to adoption support services for a recipient upon request. This only applies where the local authority has, following an assessment under section 4 of the 2002 Act, decided to provide adoption support services (*subsection (1)(a)*).

64. The local authority prepare a personal budget where they identify an amount as available to secure the adoption support services that they have decided to provide, with a view to the recipient being involved in securing those services (section 4A(3)).

65. Section 4A(4) enables regulations to be made to make detailed provision about personal budgets, including for direct payments to be made to the recipient in order for the recipient to secure the service, the provision of information, support and advice in connection with personal budgets and direct payments, and when, to whom and on what conditions direct payments may or may not be made. The first set of regulations

made under section 4A(4) will be subject to the affirmative resolution procedure (section 4A(7)).

66. If regulations authorise direct payments to be made to an adoptive parent or an adopted child they must require them to consent before the direct payment can be made. They must also require local authorities to stop making direct payments where that consent is withdrawn (section 4A(5)).

67. Any adoption support services that are secured by means of direct payments will be treated as adoption support services provided by the local authority (section 4A(6)).

Section 6: Adoption support services: duty to provide information

68. This section inserts a new section 4B into the 2002 Act.

69. Section 4B(1) places a new duty on local authorities in England to provide a range of information about adoption support services and other prescribed information to any person who has contacted the local authority to request information about adopting a child, or has informed the local authority that they wish to adopt a child. Local authorities must also provide such information to any person within their area who they are aware is the parent of an adopted child or to any such person upon request. This subsection also makes provision for regulations to prescribe the circumstances in which a local authority does not need to provide the information.

70. Section 4B(2) sets out the information that the local authority must provide including information about the adoption support services available in their area and information about assessments for adoption support services. It also makes provision for regulations to prescribe other information that must be provided by the local authority.

Section 7 and Schedule 1: The Adoption and Children Act Register

71. This section amends the provisions in the 2002 Act that provide for the establishment of an Adoption and Children Act Register ("the register") of children suitable for adoption and prospective adopters who are suitable to adopt a child.

72. *Subsection (2)* amends section 125(1)(a) of the 2002 Act to allow for the inclusion in the register of prescribed information about children who are being considered for adoption by an English local authority. This is intended to enable details of looked after children to be included in the register where the local authority are considering adoption as an option for them, or they are satisfied that the child ought to be placed for adoption but they are not authorised to do so either by parental consent or a placement order. These children may be placed with local authority foster parents who are also approved prospective adopters under new section 22C(9A) of the Children Act 1989 (see section 2). This subsection also amends section 125(3) of the 2002 Act to remove any doubt that the restriction is subject to regulations made under section 128A (as inserted by *subsection (4)*).

73. A new section 125(1A) is inserted into the 2002 Act to provide that regulations may enable the register to contain prescribed information about children that Welsh, Scottish or Northern Irish adoption agencies are satisfied are suitable for adoption and prospective adopters that they are satisfied are suitable to adopt a child (*paragraph 2(3)* of Schedule 1).

74. *Subsection (3)* amends section 128(4)(b) of the 2002 Act to provide that consent needs to be given by a prescribed person if information about a child who is being considered for adoption by an English local authority is to be disclosed to the Secretary of State or the registration organisation.

75. *Subsection (4)* inserts a new section 128A into the 2002 Act, which provides for regulations to allow for the search and inspection of the register by prospective adopters who are suitable to adopt a child to enable them to identify a child on the register for

whom they might be appropriate adopters. A prospective adopter is suitable to adopt a child if an adoption agency is satisfied that they are suitable to have a child placed with them for adoption (section 131(2)(b)). The regulations may restrict access to certain parts of the register only, or only to specified content on the register (*subsection (2)* of section 128A) and the regulations may also set out terms and conditions of access to the register (*subsection (3)* of section 128A). *Subsection (4)* of section 128A provides that regulations may prescribe the steps that prospective adopters must follow in relation to the information they have received through their search of the register. *Subsection (5)* of section 128A provides that the regulations may prescribe the payment of a fee to the Secretary of State or the registration organisation by the prospective adopters for the searching or inspecting of the register. The first set of regulations made under section 128A will be subject to the affirmative resolution procedure (*subsection (6)* of section 128A).

76. Section 129(1) of the 2002 Act is amended to provide that information entered in the register, or compiled from information entered in the register, may also be disclosed under the regulations made under section 128A of the 2002 Act (*paragraph 6* of Schedule 1). *Paragraph 6* of Schedule 1 inserts a new section 129(2A) which provides for regulations to permit the disclosure of prescribed information entered in the register or compiled from information entered in the register to adoption agencies in England, Wales, Scotland and Northern Ireland and to the registers in Scotland, Wales and Northern Ireland. Section 129(4) is amended to provide that regulations may prescribe the steps to be taken by adoption agencies in respect of information disclosed to them under new section 129(2A) and section 129(7) is amended to provide that regulations may require Welsh, Scottish or Northern Irish adoption agencies, as well as adoption agencies in England, to pay a prescribed fee in prescribed circumstances and to provide that the regulations may require any person to whom information is disclosed under new section 129(2A) to pay a prescribed fee.

77. *Subsection (5)* amends section 129(2)(a) to provide that prescribed information entered in the register may be disclosed where an adoption agency in England is acting on behalf of a child for whom they are considering adoption.

78. *Subsection (6)* amends section 140(7) to provide that subordinate legislation made under the 2002 Act may make different provision for different areas. This will enable the regulations made under section 128A to apply in certain local authority areas only.

79. *Subsection (7)* inserts a new *subsection (6A)* into section 97 of the Children Act 1989 to provide that entering information on the register under section 125 of the 2002 Act or accessing information, in accordance with any regulations made under the new section 128A of the 2002 Act, would not be an offence under section 97 of the 1989 Act.

80. *Subsection (8)* introduces Schedule 1 which amends the 2002 Act to provide for the removal of the requirement to make provision for the register by Order in Council, and for that register not to apply to Wales or Scotland.

Contact

Section 8: Contact: children in care of local authorities

81. Section 34 of the Children Act 1989 provides that where a child is in the care of the local authority the authority must allow the child reasonable contact with their parents or guardians, or certain other persons specified in section 34(1). Local authorities are also required, under *paragraph 15* of Schedule 2 to that Act, to endeavour to promote contact between all looked after children and those persons listed in *paragraph 15(1)*, including the child's parents and other relatives of the child, like grandparents or siblings. This section makes amendments to both of these provisions.

82. *Subsection (2)* amends section 34(1) to make it clear that the local authority's duty to allow reasonable contact between a child in the care of the local authority and those

people listed in section 34(1)(a) to (d) is subject to the local authority's duty to safeguard and promote the welfare of looked after children under section 22(3)(a) of the Children Act 1989. If allowing contact with any of those persons would not safeguard and promote the welfare of the child, the local authority should not allow the contact.

83. *Subsection (4)* enables the Secretary of State to make secondary legislation setting out in more detail the matters that the local authority should consider when determining whether contact between the child and any of the people mentioned in section 34(1) is consistent with safeguarding and promoting the child's welfare.

84. *Subsection (3)* inserts a new *subsection (6A)* into section 34 to provide that where a local authority in England is refusing contact under section 34(6) with any of the persons listed in section 34(1)(a) to (d), or where a local authority has obtained a court order under section 34(4) authorising them to refuse contact with any of those persons, the duty in paragraph 15(1) of Schedule 2 no longer applies.

85. Section 34(11) provides that before making a care order with respect to any child the court has to consider the contact arrangements that the local authority has made or proposes to make and invite the parties to the proceedings to comment on those arrangements. *Subsection (5)* amends that subsection to provide that the court's duties also apply before the court makes, varies or discharges an order under section 34.

Section 9: Contact: post-adoption

86. This section inserts new sections 51A and 51B into the 2002 Act which provide for the making of orders which deal with contact arrangements at the adoption order stage and subsequently between an adopted child and those persons listed in section 51A(3).

87. Section 51A provides that orders under that section can only be made where an adoption agency has placed or was authorised to place a child for adoption and the court is making, or has made an adoption order.

88. When making the adoption order or at any time afterwards the court may either make an order for contact under section 51A(2)(a) or an order prohibiting contact under section 51A(2)(b). The court may also, when making an adoption order, make an order under section 51A(2)(b) prohibiting contact on its own initiative (section 51A(6)).

89. Section 51A(3) prescribes the persons that may be made subject to an order under section 51A. These include former relatives and guardians of the child, amongst others, as well as any person who has lived with the child for at least one year. Section 51A(7) provides that the one year period need not have been continuous but must not have started more than five years before the application for an order under section 51A was made.

90. Under section 51A(4) the child, the person who has applied for the adoption order or the child's adoptive parents may make an application for an order under section 51A without the permission of the court. Any other person may apply for an order if they have obtained the permission of the court to do so.

91. Section 51A(5) sets out the factors that the court must consider when deciding whether to grant permission, under *subsection (4)(c)*, to apply for an order. It provides that the court must consider the possible harm that might be caused to the child by the proposed application, the applicant's connection to the child, and any representations that are made to them by the child, the person who has applied for the adoption order or the child's adoptive parents.

92. Section 51A(8) provides that where section 51A applies, an order under section 8 of the Children Act 1989 may not provide for contact between the child and anyone who might be named in a section 51A order. Section 26(5) of the 2002 Act is also repealed (by *subsection (3)*) to ensure that no application for a contact order under section 8 of

the Children Act 1989 may be made at the same time as an application for an adoption order.

93. An order under section 51A may contain directions on how it will be carried into effect, be made subject to appropriate conditions, be varied or revoked following an application by the child, the adoptive parents or the person named in the order under section 51A and has effect until the child's 18th birthday (section 51B(1)).

94. Section 51B(4) sets out what rules of court may specify and section 51B(3) provides that the court must, in the light of any rules made, draw up a timetable in relation to orders under section 51A and give directions for ensuring, so far as is reasonably practicable, that any timetable is adhered to.

95. Section 1(7) of the 2002 Act is amended to provide that it applies to orders made under section 51A (*subsection (2)*). This means that the requirements of section 1(2) to (4) of that Act, for example, that the welfare of the child must be the court's paramount consideration, apply when the court is considering making an order under section 51A.

96. Section 96(3) of the 2002 Act is amended to provide that it is not an offence under section 95 of that Act (which prohibits certain payments relating to adoption) to make payments for legal and/or medical expenses in relation to an application for a section 51A order (*subsection (4)*).

97. Section 1(1) of the Family Law Act 1986 ("the 1986 Act") is amended to ensure that a section 51A order is classed as a "Part 1 Order" for the purposes of Part 1 of that Act (*subsection (5)*). This enables section 51A orders to be recognised and enforced throughout the UK. Section 2 of the 1986 Act is amended to provide for the circumstances in which a court in England and Wales shall have jurisdiction to make an order under section 51A of the 2002 Act (*subsection (6)*).

98. Section 9 of the Children Act 1989 is amended to provide that a court must not make a specific issue or prohibited steps order when the same result could be achieved by making an order under section 51A (*subsection (7)*). This makes the position with regards to orders under section 51A consistent with the previous position in relation to residence and contact orders.

99. A number of sections of the Armed Forces Act 1991 ("the 1991 Act") are amended to add references to any person in whose favour an order under section 51A of the 2002 Act is in force with respect to the child, alongside references to any person named in a child arrangements order which regulates contact (under section 8 of the 1989 Act) (*subsections (8), (9), (10)* and *(11)*).

100. Paragraphs 12(9)(p) and 13(1)(g) of Part 1 of Schedule 1 to the Legal Aid, Sentencing and Punishment of Offenders Act 2012 are amended to ensure that adoption related contact orders under section 51A of the 2002 Act are within the scope of civil legal aid in the same way as orders under section 8 of the Children Act 1989.

Part 2 – FAMILY JUSTICE

Section 10: Family mediation information and assessment meetings

101. *Subsection (1)* provides that any person who wishes to make a relevant family application must first attend a family mediation information and assessment meeting (a "MIAM") to find out about and consider mediation, or other forms of non-court based dispute resolution. *Subsection (1)* does not make a distinction between applicants who are publicly funded and applicants who are not.

102. *Subsection (2)* enables provision to be made in Family Procedure Rules for how the requirement in *subsection (1)* is to work in practice. This may include provision:

- Setting out circumstances in which the requirement to attend a MIAM before making an application to court will not apply (*subsection (2)(a))*. For example, Family Procedure Rules may provide that the requirement to attend will not apply in cases where the application is urgent or where a MIAM cannot be arranged within a specified time, or where there is evidence of domestic violence.
- About how attendance at a MIAM is arranged and how a MIAM is to be conducted (*subsection (2)(b)*).
- For the court to refuse to issue or otherwise deal with an application if the requirement to attend a MIAM should have, but has not, been complied with (*subsection (2)(c)*).
- About the evidence which is to be considered when determining whether the requirement to attend a MIAM applies and, if so, whether it has been complied with (*subsection (2)(d)*).

103. *Subsection (3)* defines various terms used in *subsections (1)* and *(2)*. For example, it provides that a "relevant family application" is an application made in family proceedings that is of a description specified in Family Procedure Rules. The Government invited the Family Procedure Rule Committee to make provision in prospective Family Procedure Rules for the types of proceedings to which the MIAM requirement should apply. For example, that the requirement to attend a MIAM will apply (unless an exemption applies) in relation to an application for a child arrangements order. The FPRC is considering prospective draft rules.

104. *Subsection (4)* makes it clear that the powers in the section to make provision in Family Procedure Rules have no limiting effect on sections 75 and 76 of the Court Act 2003 (which provide the general power to make Family Procedure Rules, being rules regulating practice and procedure in family proceedings).

Section 11: ***Welfare of the child: parental involvement***

105. The purpose of this amendment to section 1 of the Children Act 1989 is to reinforce the importance of children having an ongoing relationship with both parents after family separation, where that is safe and in the child's best interests. The new subsection (2B) of section 1 is explicit that it is not the purpose of this amendment to promote the equal division of a child's time between separated parents. The effect is to require the court, in making decisions on contested section 8 orders, the contested variation or discharge of such orders or the award or removal of parental responsibility, to presume that a child's welfare will be furthered by the involvement of each of the child's parents in his or her life, unless it can be shown that such involvement would not in fact further the child's welfare. Involvement means any kind of direct or indirect involvement but not any particular division of the child's time. . (A "section 8 order" is one of the orders defined by section 8 of the Children Act 1989 - child arrangements orders (which replace contact orders and residence orders), prohibited steps orders and specific issue orders.)

106. The presumption can only apply in the case of a parent falling within the new section 1(6)(a) of the Children Act 1989. A parent falls within section 1(6)(a) if that parent can be involved in the child's life in a way that does not put the child at risk of suffering harm. A parent is to be treated (by virtue of the new section 1(6)(b)) as someone whose involvement will not give rise to a risk of harm to the child unless the court has evidence before it that involvement of that person would give rise to such a risk, whatever the form of the involvement.

107. If a parent can be involved in the child's life in a way that does not put the child at risk of suffering harm (whether that be through direct, indirect or supervised contact) the presumption applies to that parent and the court must then go on to consider whether the presumption is rebutted on the basis that it is shown that the involvement of that parent would not in fact further the child's welfare.

108. Therefore, even where a parent can be involved without posing a risk of harm to the child, the presumption will be rebutted if the court believes that the parent's involvement is not consistent with the child's welfare.

109. In a case where the presumption stands in respect of either or both of the child's parents, the court will be required to presume that the child's welfare will be furthered by the involvement of that parent (or those parents) in the child's life. This will be a consideration for the court to weigh in the balance when deciding whether to make an order (and if so what order to make) in a particular case, along with the other considerations in section 1 of the Children Act 1989, subject to the overriding requirement that the child's welfare remains the court's paramount consideration.

110. A process map and examples are set out at Annex A in order to further explain how the presumption is expected to fit with the decision making process.

Section 12: Child arrangements orders

111. *Subsection (2)* removes the definitions in section 8(1) of the Children Act 1989 of a residence order and a contact order. These orders are replaced by a child arrangements order, in line with the recommendation made by the Family Justice Review.

112. *Subsection (3)* inserts into section 8(1) of the Children Act 1989 the definition of the new child arrangements order. A child arrangements order is an order regulating arrangements relating to with whom a child should live, spend time, or have other types of contact, or when they should do so. The "other types of contact" a child arrangements order may provide for could include indirect contact such as a telephone call by the parent. As previously, specific matters which arise in connection with the exercise of parental responsibility for a child (including matters giving rise to a need to limit the exercise of that parental responsibility), and that do not relate to who the child should live with or have contact with, will be dealt with by means of a specific issue order or a prohibited steps order (as defined in section 8(1) of the Children Act 1989) as appropriate.

113. Entitlement to apply for a child arrangements order in general mirrors the previous entitlement in respect of section 8 orders. But there is one extension of that entitlement, which arises as a result of consequential amendments to sections 10 and 12 of the Children Act 1989, detailed further below.

Schedule 2 – Child arrangements orders: amendments

114. Schedule 2 consists of two Parts, each containing amendments to legislation that relate to section 12 (child arrangements orders) and, in particular, the replacement of the "residence order" and the "contact order" by the child arrangements order. In addition, certain of these amendments reflect a shift in focus in order to achieve a particular policy aim. For those provisions where this is the case, a more detailed explanation is provided below.

115. Many of these amendments are those which replace the words "residence order" or "contact order" with "child arrangements order". For many of those provisions which previously referred either to residence or contact orders, the distinction remains, but the language now reflects that the order in question will be a specific type of child arrangements order.

116. Whilst the name of the order in question will change, the rights that flow from the order will remain. If, for example, the order provides that a child shall live with a particular person, that person (or others seeking confirmation that the child lives with that person), can rely on that child arrangements order as confirmation that the child should be living with that person, in the same way as was previously the case in relation to a residence order. The content of the order will set out with whom the child is to live. From an international perspective, it is the content of an order rather than the name of the

order that is important. A child arrangements order which regulates arrangements about whom the child concerned is to live with will operate in the same way as a residence order does at present. Parental responsibility that results from the making of such an order will remain.

Schedule 2, Part 1: Amendments of the Children Act 1989

117. Part 1 of Schedule 2 contains the amendments to the Children Act 1989 that relate to section 12 (child arrangements orders). Several amendments to the Children Act 1989 have the aim of replicating, in so far as possible, the current position as regards residence orders and contact orders. However, some amendments have required additional provisions to be inserted into sections in that Act or an alteration to the focus of such sections. This is to ensure that the amendments reflect the policy aim of moving away from terminology that implies that there is a winner or loser in disputes concerning children (the perception often being that the parent with residence is the winner while the parent with contact is the loser). Where more detailed amendments have been required, further explanation is provided below.

118. Of particular note in this regard are the amendments made by *paragraphs 7* to *11* of Schedule 2 which amend sections 11A to 11E of the Children Act 1989. Sections 11A to 11E relate to "contact activity directions", which are directions that the court is able to make where it is considering making provision about contact, and "contact activity conditions", which can be imposed in a contact order. Contact activity directions and contact activity conditions have the aim of promoting contact. The amendments to sections 11A to 11E mean that the activities directed or imposed are able to relate to more than just promoting the contact provided for in the child arrangements order (or provision about contact which the court is considering). Instead the activities directed or imposed will be about helping to establish, maintain or improve the involvement of a person in a child's life. As such, these directions and conditions will no longer be referred to as "contact activity directions" or "contact activity conditions", but will be "activity directions" and "activity conditions".

119. The shift in focus here is to recognise that where the child lives with more than one person or lives with one person and spends time or otherwise has contact with another person, there may be issues that relate to the time spent by the child with the person with whom he or she lives, that affect the smooth operation of the arrangements for the care of the child. In such circumstances, these issues could be addressed by an activity direction or condition.

120. In addition, various amendments in Schedule 2 mean that the court will be able to make activity directions when it is considering whether a person has failed to comply with a provision of a child arrangements order, or what steps to take in consequence of such a failure, but where the court is not considering whether to vary or revoke the child arrangements order itself. These amendments will ensure that where there is an alleged or actual failure to comply with a child arrangements order, the court can consider whether it would help in resolving any dispute to require one or more of the adults involved to attend an activity such as a parenting information programme.

121. Sections 11F and 11G of the Children Act 1989 are supplementary to sections 11A to 11E. Sections 11H to 11P make provision as to the enforcement of contact orders and the payment of compensation where one person is in breach of an order and the other person suffers financial loss. Amendments made to these sections are to ensure that where a child arrangements order is in force with respect to a child and the provisions setting out the living arrangements (not just arrangements about contact) are sufficiently precise so that it is clear when a person is in breach of the order, the sanctions currently available to the court by virtue of sections 11H to 11P are available for breaches of a child arrangements order by any person who the child is to live with.

122. *Paragraph 21* amends section 12 of the Children Act 1989 and relates to the entitlement to parental responsibility as a result of being named in a child arrangements order. New

subsection (1A) gives the court the power to give parental responsibility to the child's father or second female parent (by virtue of section 43 of the Human Fertilisation and Embryology Act 2008) in cases where the father (or second female parent) is named in the order as a person with whom the child is to spend time or otherwise have contact.

123. New subsection (2A) enables the court to give parental responsibility to a person who is not a child's parent or guardian, in cases where a child arrangements order provides for the child concerned to spend time with or otherwise have contact (but not live) with that person. As for subsection 12(2), parental responsibility is limited to the duration of the relevant provision.

124. As a result of new section 12(2A) and new section 10(5)(d) the entitlement to apply for a child arrangements order will be extended. New paragraph (d) of section 10(5) of the Children Act 1989 (see *paragraph 5(3)(c)* of Schedule 2) provides that a person who has parental responsibility by virtue of provision under new section 12(2A) is entitled to apply for a child arrangements order. The Government considers that the extension of entitlement that would be effected by new section 10(5)(d) is narrow because there are likely to be only a few cases in which the court considers it appropriate to give parental responsibility to a person with whom a child spends time or otherwise has contact but does not live.

125. Section 14 of the Children Act 1989, which relates to measures for the enforcement of residence orders under section 63(3) of the Magistrates' Courts Act 1980, is repealed by *paragraph 23*. No equivalent is needed because the enforcement powers of the family court established by the Crime and Courts Act 2013 are sufficient.

Schedule 2, Part 2 – Child arrangements order – amendments in other legislation

126. Part 2 of Schedule 2 contains amendments to legislation other than the Children Act 1989 that relate to section 12 (child arrangements orders). Many of these amendments replace references to a "residence order" or "contact order" with a references to a "child arrangements order", and all are made either with the intention of preserving the original policy effect of the legislation concerned, or to reflect the new intentions referred to above (for example, in relation to the ability to make activity directions where there has been an alleged or actual failure to comply with a provision of a child arrangements order).

Section 13: Control of expert evidence, and of assessments, in children proceedings

127. This section makes provision about when expert evidence may be sought or put before the court in children proceedings. It is intended that, in so far as children proceedings are concerned, these measures will replace similar provisions which are contained in the new Part 25 of the Family Procedure Rules 2010 which is inserted into the 2010 Rules by the Family Procedure (Amendment) (No.5) Rules 2012 S.I. 2012/3061 and came into force on 31 January 2013. The new Part 25 is largely a consolidation of new and old rules relating to the control of expert evidence.

128. *Subsection (1)* requires that any person wishing to instruct an expert to provide evidence for use in children proceedings must first seek the permission of the court to do so; *subsection (3)* similarly requires the court's permission for a child to be medically or psychiatrically examined or otherwise assessed by an expert for the purpose of preparing expert evidence for the court; and *subsection (5)* likewise requires the court's permission for expert evidence, whether in the form of a written report or oral evidence, to be put before the court. Similar restrictions are well established in court rules and are now all set out in Part 25 of the Family Procedure Rules.

129. *Subsections (2)* and *(4)* provide for what is to happen where an expert is instructed or a child medically or psychiatrically examined or otherwise assessed to provide expert evidence for use in children proceedings without first obtaining the court's permission. In these circumstances evidence resulting from the instructions or examination or

assessment is inadmissible in children proceedings unless the court rules that it is admissible.

130. *Subsection (6)* sets out the test for permission. The court will only be able to give permission as mentioned in *subsections (1), (3)* and *(5)* if it is satisfied that the expert evidence is necessary to assist the court in resolving the proceedings justly. In reaching that decision, the court has to consider the factors specified in *subsection (7),* and any additional factors which may be prescribed by way of Family Procedure Rules. The factors have the effect, among other things, that the court will need to consider how the child might be affected if it is likely that the instruction of an expert would lengthen the timetable for the proceedings.

131. *Subsection (8)* excludes certain types of evidence from the ambit of expert evidence so they are not subject to the restrictions set out in the section. These include any evidence given by a person who is a member of staff of a local authority or of an authorised applicant. The purpose is to ensure, for example, that local authority social workers are not captured within the definition of expert evidence and permission is not required before they can provide a report or give evidence. Similarly, evidence given by officers of the Children and Family Court Advisory and Support Service (Cafcass) or Cafcass Cymru, and any evidence provided in connection with determining the suitability of a child for adoption, is not expert evidence and will not be subject to these restrictions.

132. *Subsection (9)* enables "children proceedings" to be defined in the Family Procedure Rules for the purposes of the section.

133. *Subsection (10)* is intended to ensure that any other matter relating to experts in children proceedings can continue to be determined by the Family Procedure Rules.

134. *Subsection (11)* amends section 38 of the Children Act 1989, which enables the court to give such directions as it considers appropriate relating to the medical or psychiatric examination or other assessment of the child when making an interim care order or an interim supervision order (section 38(6)). The new *subsections (7A)* and *(7B)* align section 38 with the new test for permission for expert evidence in children proceedings (as provided for in the previous provisions of section 14) so that the court may only make a direction for such an examination or assessment to be undertaken if it is satisfied that it is necessary to assist the court to resolve the proceedings justly (new *subsection 7A*). In reaching a decision, the court must consider a number of factors mirroring those in *subsection (7)* of the section *(new subsection (7B)).*

Section 14: ***Care, supervision and other family proceedings: time limits and timetables***

135. *Subsection (2)* amends section 32(1) of the Children Act 1989, which relates to the timetabling of proceedings on an application for a care or a supervision order, to require the court to timetable care and supervision cases with a view to concluding them without delay and, in any event, within 26 weeks of an application being issued.

136. *Subsection (3)* inserts a series of new subsections into section 32. New subsections (3) and (4) require that particular regard is had by the court to the impact of the timetable on the welfare of the child when drawing up the timetable for a case, revising that timetable, or making any decision (excluding an extension under new subsection (5), dealt with below) which may give rise to a revision of the timetable. The starting point for the court when timetabling cases should always be that the proceedings should be disposed of without delay, and in any event within the applicable period, which will be 26 weeks in the absence of an extension.

137. New subsection (5) of section 32 allows the court to extend the maximum case duration to be observed when timetabling an application beyond the 26 week time limit, or beyond the end of any previous extension, only if the court considers that an extension (or further extension) is necessary to enable it to resolve the proceedings justly. A

decision to extend the maximum case duration to be observed when timetabling the application will in almost every case be followed by a revision of the timetable for the case to take advantage of the extension, for example, by relisting the date of a hearing. When deciding whether to extend time, the court must have particular regard to the impact which any ensuing revision of the timetable would have on the welfare of the child to whom the application relates, or on the duration and conduct of the proceedings.

138. New subsection (7) of section 32 highlights, by way of guidance, that extensions should not be granted routinely, and should be seen as requiring specific justification.

139. The factors which may be relevant when the court is considering whether to extend time beyond 26 weeks, or beyond the end of a previous extension may include, for example, the disability or other impairment of a person involved in the proceedings, if that means that their involvement in the case requires more time than it otherwise would, or external factors beyond the court's control, such as parallel criminal proceedings, if that is relevant to the case.

140. New subsection (8) of section 32 provides that each separate extension of time made under *subsection (5)* is to last no more than 8 weeks (even where an extension is granted after the expiry of the period being extended).

141. New subsection (9) of section 32 gives the Lord Chancellor power by making regulations to vary the 26 week time limit or the 8 week time limit for extensions. Such regulations would be subject to the affirmative procedure by virtue of amendments contained in section 16(1).

142. New subsection (10) of section 32 provides for rules of court (Family Procedure Rules) to be able to make certain provision relating to the matters to which the court should have regard when deciding whether to extend the time limit to be observed when timetabling for disposal of an application.

143. *Subsection (4)(a)* removes the limits on the duration of interim care orders (ICOs) and interim supervision orders (ISOs) set out in section 38 of the Children Act 1989 (8 weeks for initial orders and 4 weeks for any subsequent orders). Instead the judge will be able to set the length of ICOs and ISOs for a period which is considered appropriate in the particular circumstances of the case, although no ICO or ISO can endure beyond the cessation of the proceedings themselves. Should an ICO or an ISO expire before the proceedings have been resolved, the court will be able to make a further order.

144. It is expected that when making an ICO or ISO it will usually be appropriate to align the duration of the ICO or ISO with the timetable for the proceedings (including any extensions that may have been granted), to avoid the need for the court to make multiple ICOs or ISOs within proceedings.

145. *Subsection (7)* makes minor amendments to section 32(1) of the Children Act 1989. *Subsection (7)(b)* clarifies that a court is required to draw up a timetable in the light of any provision in rules of court that is of the kind mentioned in subsection (2)(a) or (b) (whether or not the rules themselves are made by virtue of subsection (2)).

146. *Subsection (5), (6)* and *(8)* are consequential upon the change in wording contained within *subsection (7)*.

*Section 15: **Care Plans***

147. This section amends section 31 of the Children Act 1989 so as to focus the court's consideration, when making its decision as to whether to make a care order, on the provisions of the care plan that set out the long term plan for the upbringing of the child. Specifically, the court is to consider whether the local authority care plan is for the child to live with a parent or any member or friend of the child's family, or whether the child is to be adopted or placed in other long term care. These are referred to as the "permanence provisions" of the section 31A plan. The court is not required to consider

the remainder of the section 31A plan (subject to section 34(11) which requires the court to consider the contact arrangements for the child), although the amendments do not prevent the court from doing so.

148. New subsection (3C) of section 31 provides that the Secretary of State may by regulations amend what is meant by the "permanence provisions".

Section 16: Care proceedings and care plans: regulations: procedural requirements

149. This section is consequential on the previous two sections and provides that regulations made under either section 31(3C) (regulations about permanence provisions) or 32(9) (regulations amending time limits for disposal of care or supervision proceedings) of the Children Act 1989 are to be subject to an affirmative resolution procedure.

Section 17: Repeal of restrictions on divorce and dissolution etc where there are children

150. This section repeals section 41 of the Matrimonial Causes Act 1973 and section 63 of the Civil Partnership Act 2004 which require the court to consider whether it should exercise any of its powers under the Children Act 1989 in proceedings for a decree of divorce, nullity of marriage, or judicial separation or, in relation to a civil partnership, for a dissolution, nullity or separation order. These sections apply where there are children under the age of 16 or where there are children who have reached the age of 16 to whom the court directs that the provisions should apply.

151. Where there are disputes over children or financial issues, the parties are able to make an application under the relevant section of the Children Act 1989 or the Matrimonial Causes Act 1973 (or the Civil Partnership Act 2004 for civil partnerships). Arrangements for children will no longer be scrutinised as part of the divorce process but can instead be resolved through separate proceedings at any time.

152. *Subsection (1)* repeals the relevant sections of the 1973 and 2004 Acts and *subsections (2)* to *(7)* make consequential amendments and repeals in respect of provisions in the Matrimonial Causes Act 1973, the Children Act 1989 and the Civil Partnership Act 2004.

Section 18: Repeal of uncommenced provisions of Part 2 of the Family Law Act 1996

153. This section repeals uncommenced provisions of Part 2 of the Family Law Act 1996. The Family Law Act 1996 received Royal Assent on 4 July 1996. Part 2 of the 1996 Act introduced revised divorce procedures and encouraged people to consider using mediation to resolve disputes arising on divorce.

154. *Subsection (1)* repeals the uncommenced divorce provisions contained in Part 2 of the Family Law Act 1996. Section 22 (funding of marriage support services) is in force and is not being repealed.

155. *Subsection (2)* repeals various provisions of the Family Law Act 1996 which relate to the provisions of Part 2, including the general principle in section 1(c) relating to bringing marriage to an end with minimum distress to the parties and to encouraging family mediation. A range of non-statutory initiatives pre-court and at court have been introduced to promote and encourage consideration and use of mediation and these are aimed at all separating parents, whether or not the parents are married.

156. *Subsection (3)* makes consequential repeals of other legislation.

157. *Subsections (4)* and *(5)* make consequential amendments.

158. *Subsections (6)* and *(7)* turn modifications to statutory provisions, which were contained in commencement orders and were to have effect until such time as provisions of

Part 2 of the Family Law Act 1996 came into force, into permanent amendments to the modified provisions. For example, certain modifications to section 22(2) of the Matrimonial and Family Law Proceedings Act 1984 made by a commencement order are to be made permanent.

159. *Subsection (8)* makes minor amendments to section 31(7D) of the Matrimonial Causes Act 1973 which is one of the provisions for which modifications are made permanent by *subsection (7)*.

160. *Subsection (9)* defines the commencement orders referred to in this section and revokes the provisions of these orders which contain the modifications to statutes which are being turned into permanent amendments by *subsections (6) and (7)* or which are no longer needed.

PART 3 - children and young people in england with special Educational Needs OR DISABILITIES

Local authority functions: general principles

Section 19: Local authority functions: Supporting and involving children and young people

161. This section sets out the general principles that local authorities must have regard to in exercising their powers and duties under Part 3 of the Act in the case of children and young people. The principles are based on the Government's vision for reforming services for children and young people with special educational needs, as set out in the 2011 Green Paper, *Support and Aspiration: A new approach to Special Educational Needs and Disability*. They seek to ensure that local authorities place children, young people and families at the centre of decision making, enable them to participate in a fully informed way, and with a focus on achieving the best possible outcomes.

Special educational needs etc

Section 20: When a child or young person has special educational needs

162. A child or young person has special educational needs if they have a learning difficulty or disability which calls for special educational provision to be made for them.

163. Children and young people with special educational needs may require extra or different provision in relation to thinking and understanding, as a result of physical or sensory difficulties, emotional or behavioural difficulties, difficulties with speech and language or how they relate to and behave with other people. Disabled children and young people may require extra or different provision, for example, if they are less mobile than their peers and require additional or extra provision so they can access the same learning opportunities.

164. A child or young person does not have a learning difficulty or disability simply because the language in which they are (or will be) taught is different from the one they speak at home.

165. This section replicates the current definition of special educational needs in section 312 of the Education Act 1996 and the definition of a learning difficulty in section 15Z(6) and (7) of the Education Act 1996, applying a single definition to children and young people from birth to 25.

166. Section 83 defines various terms:

- Young person is a person over compulsory school age[1] but under 25.

---

1 *Compulsory school age* has the meaning given by section 8 of the Education Act 1996. A person begins to be of compulsory school age when he attains the age of 5 on 31st March, 31st August or 31st December in any year, or where he attains the age

- Child is a person who is not over compulsory school age: see section 579 of the Education Act 1996.
- Mainstream schools are maintained schools and Academy schools that are not special schools. A maintained school is a community, foundation or voluntary school, or a community or foundation special school not established in a hospital.
- Post-16 institution is any institution that provides education or training for those over compulsory school age, but which is not a school or within the higher education sector. Mainstream post-16 institutions are those which are not specially organised to make special educational provision for students with special educational needs, that is, further education colleges, sixth form colleges, 16-19 Academies and training providers. Special post-16 institutions are post-16 institutions that are specially organised to make special educational provision for students with special educational needs. They are not within the further education sector or 16-19 Academies and are currently often referred to as independent specialist providers or independent specialist colleges.

Section 21: Special educational provision, health care provision and social care provision

167. This section defines special educational provision, health care provision and social care provision.

168. Special educational provision is additional or different from that which would normally be provided for children or young people of the same age in mainstream schools or colleges, maintained nursery schools and places at which relevant early years education is provided. It might include support from a specialist teacher, access to a specialist teaching programme, specialist ICT equipment or a specialist job coach. For children under two it means educational provision of any kind.

169. Health care provision means provision of health care services provided as part of the NHS. These services may be provided by or on behalf of NHS bodies including by private providers. Social care provision is provision made by local authority social services. Health care provision or social care provision which educates or trains the child or young person is to be treated as special educational provision (rather than health care or social care provision). This reflects the precedents set by case law in relation to the current special educational needs legislation.

170. The section replicates, and replaces in England, the current definition of special educational provision in section 312 of the Education Act 1996 and applies it to young people over compulsory school age.

171. Relevant early years education is defined in the section as having the same meaning as under section 123 of the Schools Standards and Framework Act 1998, that is, free early years provision (as defined in section 20 of the Childcare Act 2006) which is provided under arrangements made by a local authority pursuant to section 7 of the Childcare Act 2006.

Identifying children and young people with special educational needs and disabilities

Section 22: Identifying children and young people with special educational needs and disabilities

172. This section places a duty on local authorities to identify all those children and young people in their area who have or may have special educational needs or disabilities.

---

of 5 on another date, he begins to be of compulsory school age on whichever of those dates comes next after his fifth birthday. He ceases to be of compulsory school age on the last Friday in June of the school year in which he attains the age of 16.

Children and young people can be brought to the attention of the local authority by their parents, their school or college, or other professionals, for example a social worker, General Practitioner, health visitor, teacher, early years professional or a further education tutor.

173. This section is based on, but differs from, sections 13(5) and 321 of the Education Act 1996 and will apply in England. The Education Act provisions will be repealed in relation to England when these provisions come into force.

Section 23: Duty of health bodies to bring certain children to local authority's attention

174. The section replicates section 332 of the Education Act 1996 and extends it to disabled children. Where a clinical commissioning group (CCG), NHS Trust or NHS Foundation Trust, in carrying out their functions in relation to a child under compulsory school age, are of the opinion that the child has or probably has special educational needs or a disability they must tell the child's parents and give them the chance to discuss this with an officer of the group or trust. They must then tell the appropriate local authority. They must also tell the parent if they think a particular voluntary organisation is likely to be able to give them advice or assistance in respect of their child's special educational needs or disability. This section helps to ensure that young children who may need special educational provision or information and support in relation to a disability are brought to the local authority's attention early on.

Children and young people for whom a local authority is responsible

Section 24: When a local authority is responsible for a child or young person

175. This section specifies the children and young people for whom a local authority is responsible for the purposes of Part 3 of the Act. These functions include identifying and assessing a child or young person's education, health and care needs and drawing up an EHC plan to meet them, and preparing a local offer of services that are available for children and young people with special educational needs and their families.

176. A local authority is responsible for a child or young person if he or she is in the authority's area and he or she has been identified by the authority or brought to its attention as someone who has or may have special educational needs. This will cover children and young people who live in the authority's area and are educated within it and those who live in the authority's area but who are educated outside its area. This would include, for example, children and young people with an EHC plan from the local authority's area who the authority has placed in an independent school or post-16 Independent Specialist College. This section allows anyone to bring a child to the attention of the local authority as having or possibly having special educational needs. Explicit rights for parents and young people and schools and colleges to request a statutory assessment, carried forward from the present SEN system, are set out in section 36.

177. This section replaces, in England, section 321 of the Education Act 1996 and section 139B(4) of the Learning and Skills Act 2000. Section 81 makes clear that references in this Part to a child or young person who is in the area of a local authority in England do not include a child or young person who is wholly or mainly resident in the area of a local authority in Wales.

Education, health and care provision: integration and joint commissioning

Section 25: Promoting integration

178. Local authorities are required to carry out their functions under Part 3 in a way that promotes integration between educational and training provision with health care provision and social care provision where they consider that this would promote

the well-being of children or young people who have special educational needs or a disability or where it would improve the quality of special educational provision for children and young people with special educational needs (as described in *subsection (1)*).

179. This section is intended to assist children and young people with educational, health and social care needs by improving the way services work together to provide support for them.

180. This section reflects the duty placed on CCGs by section 14Z1 of the National Health Service Act 2006 (as inserted by section 26 of the Health and Social Care Act 2012) and the proposed duty on local authorities under clause 3 of the Care Bill which look to improve integrated working between services.

*Section 26: **Joint commissioning arrangements***

181. This section requires the local authority and its partner commissioning bodies to make arrangements about the education, health and care provision to be secured for children and young people with special educational needs for whom it is responsible and for those with disabilities. Those must include arrangements for considering and agreeing the education, health and care provision reasonably required by the learning difficulties and disabilities which result in the children and young people for whom the authority is responsible having special educational needs and by the disabilities of the children and young people in its area. It does not specify the form which the arrangements should take as this should be agreed locally.

182. Commissioning Bodies are defined to include the NHS Commissioning Board as well as the individual CCGs, so the arrangements may cover circumstances in which the Board is responsible for commissioning services directly, such as low incidence/high need specialist services, and for particular groups for whom it has commissioning responsibility, such as the children of members of the armed forces. Each body which is under a duty to arrange for the provision of services and facilities under the National Health Service Act 2006 for children and young people for whom a local authority is responsible will be a partner commissioning body of the authority. *Subsection (9)* provides a power to prescribe the circumstances in which a CCG is not to be treated as a partner commissioning body.

183. The joint commissioning arrangements must include arrangements for the local authority and commissioning bodies to consider and agree the special educational, health and social care provision required locally, and to determine what provision is to be secured and by whom, in order to meet that need. The arrangements must also cover what information and advice is to be provided about education, health and care provision, how it is to be provided, and how complaints about education, health and care provision may be made and handled. In addition, the arrangements will also include procedures for resolving disputes between the partners.

184. The joint commissioning arrangements are also intended to help support other provisions. It is anticipated that the arrangements will help the local authority better inform its local offer (see section 30), help those children and young people who have special educational, health and social care needs by ensuring that there are adequate and "joined up" assessments under section 36, help secure the provision included in EHC plans, and help in agreeing personal budgets for providing support (see section 49). The local authority and its partner commissioning bodies are required to act consistently with the joint commissioning arrangements and to keep them under review so they can be updated where necessary.

185. The duty under joint commissioning arrangements may be fulfilled by making use of existing local arrangements where they are used to meet the purposes set out under this section. Such arrangements will include joint strategic needs assessments and joint health and wellbeing strategies developed pursuant to sections 116 and 116A of the

Local Government and Public Involvement in Health Act 2007 (as amended by sections 192 and 193 of the Health and Social Care Act 2012).

Review of education and care provision

Section 27: Duty to keep education and care provision under review

186. This section requires local authorities in England to keep under review the educational and training provision and social care provision made in their area for children and young people with special educational needs or disabilities and the provision made outside their area for children and young people with special educational needs for whom they are responsible and for those with disabilities.

187. Local authorities must consider the extent of provision and whether it is sufficient to meet children and young people's educational needs, training needs and social care needs. This complements the local authority's duties under section 14 and section 15ZA of the Education Act 1996 to secure sufficient schools and suitable education and training for young people.

188. When keeping their provision under review local authorities are required to consult with children and young people with special educational needs and disabilities, parents of children with special educational needs and disabilities, the bodies named in *subsection (3)* of the section and any other such people as the local authority thinks appropriate.

189. In carrying out their duties under this section local authorities must have regard to the relevant Joint Strategic Needs Assessment and Health and Well-being Strategy.

190. This section replaces section 315 of the Education Act 1996 in England and will operate alongside section 26 on joint commissioning to provide the local authority with relevant information with which to prepare the local offer.

Co-operation and assistance

Section 28: Co-operating generally: local authority functions

191. This section is a reciprocal duty of co-operation which requires local authorities and partners (listed in *subsection (2)*) to co-operate with one another in the exercise of the authority's functions in this Part relating to children and young people with special educational needs.

192. The local authority must under *subsection (3)* ensure that there is co-operation between its officers involved in education and training and social services and any other officers who assist children or young people to prepare for adulthood and independent living as part of the local offer.

193. *Subsection (4)* provides a power to prescribe the circumstances in which a CCG is not to be treated as a partner of a local authority.

Section 29: Co-operating generally: governing body functions

194. This section complements the duty in section 28, and relates to the functions of governing bodies, proprietors and management committees, rather than local authorities. It requires co-operation between those institutions listed in *subsection (2)* and local authorities in the delivery of their duties set out in these provisions.

Information and advice

Section 30: Local offer

195. This section requires local authorities to publish information about services they expect to be available for children and young people with special educational needs and disabilities. This will be called the "local offer" and local authorities will keep their local offer under review and revise it. The local offer must include information about the provision the local authority expects to be available in its own area for children and young people with special educational needs and disabilities and outside its area for those children and young people, regardless of whether or not they have EHC plans. Information about provision outside the local authority's area could include, for example, specialist provision located in a neighbouring authority but which is available to children and young people in its area.

196. The local offer will cover special educational, health care and social care provision, other educational provision, training provision, provision to assist in preparing children and young people for adulthood and independent living (such as finding employment or obtaining accommodation), arrangements for children and young people to travel to schools or post-16 education (including further education colleges, sixth form colleges, independent specialist providers and training providers) and providers of relevant early years education.

197. Regulations will set out the information local authorities should include in their local offer, how it is to be published, who is to be consulted in preparing it and how the authority will involve children and young people with special educational needs and disabilities and parents of children with special educational needs and disabilities in preparing and reviewing it. This involvement will include publishing comments about the local offer that have been received from or on behalf of those children and young people and parents, and the authority's responses to those comments, including any action it intends to take. Local authorities will also have to include information about how to seek an assessment for an EHC plan, about other sources of information, advice and support, and about how to make a complaint about provision in the local offer. The regulations will also set out the extent of the information local authorities should include about provision outside their area. Local authorities will be free to include other information in their local offer if they wish. This section on the local offer works alongside section 27 which requires local authorities to keep their education and social care provision for children and young people with special educational needs and disabilities under review, and also section 26 which requires local authorities to make joint commissioning arrangements with partner clinical commissioning groups.

Section 31: Co-operating in specific cases: local authority functions

198. This section supplements the duties in section 28 and 29. It requires health service partners, other local authorities, the person in charge of any relevant youth accommodation, and youth offending teams to co-operate when asked by a local authority for help in carrying out its duties towards children and young people with special educational needs.

199. Requests for cooperation could be in relation to assessments of individual children's special educational needs and preparation of EHC plans. Regulations may impose time limits where a request to co-operate relates to local authority duties in these areas.

200. This section replaces, in England, section 322 of the Education Act 1996.

Section 32: Advice and information

201. This section requires local authorities to make arrangements for advice and information about special educational needs and disabilities to be provided for children, young

people and the parents of children in its area with those needs, and to make the services provided known to those people, schools, colleges and others they consider appropriate.

202. This section replaces and extends section 332A of the Education Act 1996 under which local authorities have provided parent partnership services which already provide information and advice to parents of children with special educational needs. Section 332A related to children, parents and schools. The section extends the reach of the provision in section 332A to children and young people with SEN, disabled children and their parents and disabled young people. It places a duty on local authorities to make these provisions known to the head teachers, proprietors and principals of schools and post-16 institutions in their area. The local authority may also inform anyone else it thinks is appropriate.

Mainstream education

Section 33: Children and young people with EHC plans

203. Section 33 sets out what action should be taken when a local authority is making an EHC plan for a child or young person with special educational needs who is to go to a school or college, where either:

- The child's parents or the young person do not ask for a particular school or college to be named in the EHC plan in accordance with section 38; or
- The child's parents or the young person do make a request, but the local authority does not intend to name the requested provider.

204. It places a duty on the local authority to make sure that the EHC plan provides for the child or young person to be educated in a maintained nursery school or mainstream setting (that is, not in a special school or special college) unless that is against the wishes of the young person or the child's parent, or would damage the efficient education of others and there are no reasonable steps that could be taken to overcome this. If one of those conditions applies, the child or young person's EHC plan can provide for them to be educated in a special school or a special post-16 institution such as an independent specialist provider.

205. This section replaces sections 316 and 316A of the Education Act 1996 and extends the provisions to young people in post-16 education.

Section 34: Children and young people with special educational needs but no EHC plan

206. This section applies to a child or young person in England who has special educational needs but no EHC plan and who is to be educated in a school or post-16 institution. It sets out the general principle that those children and young people must be educated in a maintained nursery school, mainstream school or mainstream college except in particular circumstances. These are: where it is agreed that they are admitted to a special school or special post-16 institution to be assessed for an EHC plan; it is agreed that they are admitted to a special school or special post-16 institution following a change in their circumstances; they are admitted to a special school which is established in a hospital; or where they are admitted to a Special Academy whose Academy arrangements allow it to admit children or young people with special educational needs who do not have an EHC plan.

207. This section replaces sections 316 and 316A of the Education Act 1996 and extends the provisions to young people in post-16 education.

Section 35: Children with special educational needs in maintained nurseries and mainstream schools

208. When a child with special educational needs is being educated in a maintained nursery school or a mainstream school, the school must enable the child to take part in the activities of the school with other children as far as is reasonably practicable and so long as this ensures the child gets the special educational provision they need, does not damage the education of the other children and does not mean an inefficient use of resources.

209. This section replaces, in England, section 317(4) of the Education Act 1996.

Assessment

Section 36: Assessment of education, health and care needs

210. This section gives a child's parent, a young person or a person acting on behalf of a school or post-16 institution the right to request a statutory assessment. It requires local authorities to consider whether an assessment is necessary for a child or young person where such a request has been made or where the authority has become responsible for the child or young person in some other way, such as by someone else bringing the child or young person to the authority's attention. The section sets out the local authority's duties when making their decision about whether to carry out an assessment and in carrying out any subsequent assessment of the child or young person. In making a decision on whether an assessment is necessary, the local authority must consult with the child's parents or the young person, to ensure they are involved in the process from the outset. If the local authority decides not to carry out an assessment they must inform the child's parents or the young person of their decision and their reasons for it. If they intend to carry out an education, health and care needs assessment they must inform the child's parents or the young person and make sure that they are aware of their rights to have their own views considered by the local authority (either orally or in writing).

211. The local authority must carry out an assessment if, after taking account of any views expressed and evidence submitted, it thinks that the child or young person has or may have special educational needs and that it may be necessary for special educational provision to be made for a child or young person through an EHC plan. The parent or young person should be informed of the outcome of the assessment and whether the local authority intends to prepare an EHC plan. Further detail about the assessment process will be set out in regulations, including, for example, how assessments are conducted and advice obtained, how parents and young people can express their views and submit evidence, and about the provision of information, advice and support in connection with an assessment.

212. Section 51 provides that if, having received and considered a request for an assessment, a local authority decides not to carry one out, the child's parents or the young person may appeal against that decision to the First-tier Tribunal.

213. The provision in section 36(10) is intended to make clear that when a local authority is deciding whether to carry out an assessment for a young person aged 19 or over, it must consider whether the young person needs more time, in comparison to the majority of people their age who do not have special educational needs, to complete their education or training. Young people may have an EHC plan up to age 25 but, as young people will be ready to leave education or training and make the transition into adult life at differing ages, in many cases an EHC plan will end sooner than that.

214. This section replaces, in England, sections 323 and 331 of the Education Act 1996 and sections 139A to 139C of the Learning and Skills Act 2000.

Education, health and care plans

Section 37: Education, health and care plans

215. This section sets out what a local authority must do if the education, health and care assessment in section 36 indicates that a child or young person requires an EHC plan for their special educational provision.

216. The local authority is under a duty to make sure that an EHC plan is prepared and then implemented. The EHC plan should specify the short and long term outcomes that it is designed to help the child or young person to achieve and the special educational, health and social care provision that will be made to support them. This could include, for example, access to specialist teaching, speech and language therapy provision, and short breaks.

217. The health care provision to be specified in the EHC plan is that which is reasonably required by the learning difficulties and disabilities which result in the child or young person having special educational needs. For example, health provision could include therapies, such as occupational therapy, and equipment, such as wheelchairs and continence supplies (see also section 21).

218. The social care provision to be specified in the EHC plan includes any social care provision which must be made for a child or young person under 18 by the local authority as a result of section 2 of the Chronically Sick and Disabled Persons Act 1970. This could include practical assistance in the home or providing an outing for a child.

219. The social care provision to be specified in the EHC plan also includes other social care provision which is reasonably required by the learning difficulty or disability which results in the child or young person having special educational needs. This may include provision made under section 17 of the Children Act which is not covered by the Chronically Sick and Disabled Persons Act 1970, for example residential short breaks. It may also include adult social care provision for young people aged 18-25 with EHC plans.

220. Other health and social care provision may be included in plans, where local authorities and health commissioners consider this would be beneficial to the child or young person. For example, if a child with an EHC plan for significant dyslexia developed an unrelated illness, it might make sense for them, their parents and the professionals supporting them to co-ordinate their care through the EHC plan.

221. Further detail about the preparation (including time limits), content and maintenance of an EHC plan may be set out in regulations.

222. This section replaces, in England, section 324 of the Education Act 1996.

Section 38: Preparation of EHC plans: draft plan

223. This section sets out the process that must be undertaken by a local authority when preparing a draft EHC plan. The local authority must consult with the child's parents or the young person, to ensure they are involved in the planning process from the outset and their views are taken into account. The local authority must send a copy of the draft EHC plan to the child's parent or the young person and make sure that they are aware of the ways in which they can express their views on the content of the draft EHC plan.

224. The draft EHC plan must not name a specific institution or a type of institution. This is so that parents or young people have the opportunity to request (before the end of the time period which is specified in the notice sent to the parent or young person under *subsection (2)(b)*) that a particular school, further education college in England or other institution is named in the EHC plan before it is finalised. Parents and young people may request any institution of the types listed in *subsection (3)*. Parents and young people will also be able make representations for an independent school or post-16 independent

specialist provider not included in this list as is the case under the current legislative framework (although there will be no corresponding duty on the local authority to name such an institution in the EHC plan or for that institution to be under a duty to admit the child or young person). Local authorities may also specify education otherwise than in a school or post-16 institution in an EHC plan where they consider this to be suitable provision.

225. This section replaces, in England, section 323 of the Education Act 1996.

Section 39: Finalising EHC plans: request for particular school or other institution

226. This section applies where the child's parent or the young person has received a draft EHC plan and requested that a particular institution is named in the EHC plan.

227. The local authority is required to consult any institution that it is considering naming in the EHC plan and, where that institution is maintained by another local authority, the other authority. The local authority must comply with the parent or young person's request unless the child or young person's attendance at the school would not meet their special educational needs, or would be incompatible with the efficient education of others or the efficient use of resources. If it believes that these circumstances apply, the local authority must name the school or other institution, or type of institution, that the local authority considers to be most appropriate for the child or young person (having consulted that institution before naming it in the EHC plan). A copy of the final EHC plan must then be sent to the child's parent or the young person and to the school, college or other institution that has been named in the EHC plan.

228. This section replaces, in England, section 324 and parts of Schedule 27 of the Education Act 1996.

Section 40: Finalising EHC plans: no request for particular school or other institution

229. This section applies where the child's parent or young person has received a draft EHC plan but has not made a request for a particular institution in accordance with section 38(2)(b)(ii). They may have said they would like an independent school, training provider or early years education provider to be named, or they may have indicated no preference at all.

230. In this eventuality, the EHC plan must name the specific institution or type of institution that the local authority considers appropriate. The local authority must consult any school or institution that it is considering naming, and where that institution is maintained by another local authority, that authority, before finalising the EHC plan. A copy of the final EHC plan must then be sent to the child's parent or the young person and the school or other institution named in the EHC plan.

231. Further duties on the local authority which apply in these circumstances are set out in section 33 (duty to educate within the mainstream sector).

232. This section replaces, in England, section 324 of the Education Act 1996.

Section 41: Independent special schools and special post-16 institutions: approval

233. Independent schools that are specially organised to make special educational provision for children with special educational needs, and special post-16 institutions (independent specialist colleges) can be named in an EHC plan. This section gives the Secretary of State the power to approve such institutions and once he has done so parents and young people can express a preference for them under section 38(2), with the resultant conditional duty on the local authority to name the institution in the EHC plan. Approval can only be given if the institution consents. The Secretary of State may withdraw approval and regulations may make provision about the types of institution that can be approved, and the criteria that must be met for such approval. Regulations

may also set out the matters to be taken into account in deciding whether to give or withdraw approval and may cover publication of a list of institutions that have been approved by the Secretary of State.

*Section 42: **Duty to secure special educational provision and health care provision in accordance with EHC plan***

234. Where an EHC plan is maintained for a child or young person, the local authority must make sure that the special educational provision set out in it is made. The local authority need not make the special educational provision set out in the EHC plan if the child's parent or the young person makes alternative, suitable arrangements.

235. The responsible commissioning body must make sure that any health provision set out in the EHC plan is made. The "responsible commissioning body" in relation to any specified health care provision means the body (or each body) that is under a duty to arrange the health care provision for the child or young person. This will typically be the relevant clinical commissioning group but may also be the NHS Commissioning Board. The responsible commissioning body need not make the health provision set out in the EHC plan if the child's parent or the young person makes alternative, suitable arrangements.

236. This section replaces and expands, in England, section 324 of the Education Act 1996.

*Section 43: **Schools and other institutions named in EHC plan: duty to admit***

237. Where a maintained school, maintained nursery school, Academy, institution in the English further education sector (a further education college or sixth form college), non-maintained special school or independent school or independent specialist college approved by the Secretary of State under section 41 is named in an EHC plan it must admit the child or young person.

238. This section replaces, in England, section 324 of the Education Act 1996.

*Section 44: **Reviews and re-assessments***

239. This section requires local authorities to review a child or young person's EHC plan at least every 12 months. It also sets out when re-assessments must take place. A review is intended to consider whether the provision in the EHC plan is meeting the child or young person's assessed needs and whether they are making progress towards the outcomes identified. A re-assessment means undertaking the assessment process in section 36 again, for example when a child or young person's needs may have changed significantly. Local authorities must consult with the parent of the child, or the young person, during any review or re-assessment to ensure they are involved in the process from the outset and their views are taken into account.

240. The local authority must carry out a re-assessment if one is requested by the child's parent, the young person or the school, college or other institution that they attend, subject to particular exemptions to be set out in regulations (which might include for example where a previous assessment has been conducted relatively recently). The local authority also has the power to carry out a re-assessment without waiting for one to be requested by a parent or school.

241. In reviewing an EHC plan maintained for a young person aged 19 or over, or deciding whether to reassess their needs the local authority must have regard to whether the educational or training outcomes specified in the plan have been achieved. Many young people will have completed their education and made a successful transition to adulthood before 25. However an EHC plan can remain in place for those who need longer to complete or consolidate their learning to enable them to make a successful transition to adulthood.

242. More detail about the process for reviewing, amending or replacing EHC plans will be provided in regulations including circumstances in which a local authority must or may review an EHC plan (for example, before the end of a specified phase of a child or young person's education, or when a young person becomes NEET, that is, they are not in education, employment or training).

243. This section replaces, in England, section 323 of the Education Act 1996.

Section 45: Ceasing to maintain an EHC plan

244. A local authority may only stop maintaining an EHC plan if they are no longer responsible for that child or young person, for example if the child or young person has moved to another area, or they consider that it is no longer necessary for the EHC plan to be maintained.

245. The section sets out some of the circumstances under which it would no longer be necessary to maintain the EHC plan, for example, where the child or young person no longer requires the special educational provision specified in the EHC plan.

246. When determining that a young person aged 19 or over no longer requires special educational provision, the local authority must have regard to whether the educational or training outcomes specified in the EHC plan have been achieved. This enables a local authority to continue an EHC plan where a young person has dropped out of education (i.e. is not in education, employment or training (NEET)) but would like to return to education or training. Regulations may make further provisions about ceasing to maintain an EHC plan.

247. When an appeal is made against a local authority's decision to cease an EHC plan, the authority must continue to maintain the EHC plan until the time has passed for bringing an appeal or the appeal has been determined by the First tier Tribunal.

Section 46: Maintaining an EHC plan after young person's 25th birthday

248. This section gives local authorities the power to maintain an EHC plan for a young person until the end of the academic year (such date to be prescribed in regulations) in which they become 25, enabling them to take account of individual needs and circumstances.

Section 47: Transfer of EHC plans

249. This section enables regulations to be made regarding the process for transfers of EHC plans, when a child or young person with an EHC plan moves between local authority areas. This may include a duty on the new local authority to maintain an EHC plan prepared by the previous local authority.

250. This section replaces, in relation to England, paragraph 7(2) of Schedule 27 to the Education Act 1996.

Section 48: Release of a child or young person for whom EHC plan previously maintained

251. If a child or young person who is released from a custodial sentence previously had an EHC plan, or if the local authority is keeping a plan for them under section 70 the local authority that is responsible for the child or young person on their release (which may not be the same local authority that secured the EHC plan originally) must maintain the previous EHC plan and review it as soon as is practicable after release.

Section 49: Personal budgets and direct payments

252. This section requires local authorities to prepare a personal budget for children or young people for whom the local authority maintains an EHC plan or has decided to make

an EHC plan, if asked to do so by the child's parent or the young person. A personal budget is an amount available to secure particular provision set out in the EHC plan and provides a way of involving parents or young people in securing that provision.

253. Personal budgets can take the form of direct payments which families can spend themselves or notional budgets which they can devise with the local authority and which the local authority can spend on their behalf at their direction by arranging the provision in the EHC plan – or a combination of both.

254. Regulations will provide details about personal budgets, including provision that may be included in a personal budget or to which a direct payment may relate, the provision of information, support and advice in connection with personal budgets and direct payments, and when, to whom and on what conditions direct payments may or may not be made. Any regulations which authorise direct payments to a parent or a young person must require them to consent before a direct payment can be made. They must also require local authorities to stop making direct payments where that consent is withdrawn.

255. Special educational provision purchased with a direct payment will be treated as provision secured by the local authority for the purposes of fulfilling its duty under section 42(2) to secure the special educational provision in an EHC plan and health care provision purchased with a direct payment will be treated as provision arranged by the commissioning body for the purposes of fulfilling its duty under section 42(3).

Section 50: Continuation of services under section 17 of the Children Act 1989

256. This section inserts a new provision (section 17ZG) into the Children Act 1989.

257. It gives a power to local authorities to continue to provide services they have been providing to a young person before their 18th birthday under section 17 of the Children Act 1989 (services to children in need, their families and others) to the young person when they are 18 and over, where the young person has an EHC plan. The local authority retains discretion over how long it chooses to provide services under section 17 while an EHC plan remains in place. Where the young person no longer has an EHC plan, the local authority no longer has the power to extend the provision of these services to young people over 18.

258. The provision in this section aims to support better transitions between children's and adult services for young people with EHC plans. Guidance on how an authority should use this discretion will be set out in the Code of Practice issued under section 77.

Appeals, mediation and dispute resolution

Section 51: Appeals

259. This section sets out the decisions taken by a local authority in relation to assessments and EHC plans against which a parent or young person can appeal. These are set out in *subsection (2)*.

260. This section extends the current right of appeal to the First-tier Tribunal to young people aged up to 25 and, in the case of young people in school, transfers the right from the parent to the young person. The section also extends the right of appeal to the Tribunal to the parents of children under 2 years of age.

261. An appeal can only be made after mediation has been considered and, where the parent or young person has decided to take part in mediation, this has taken place in accordance with section 52. The Secretary of State may make regulations in relation to appeals. The Secretary of State's powers include the power to make regulations giving the Tribunal the power to make recommendations about the health and social care elements of EHC plans in pilot areas (see section 51(4)(a)).

262. *Subsection (5)* recreates an offence, carried over from the Education Act 1996. A person commits an offence if, without reasonable excuse, they fail to comply with any requirement to provide or allow for inspection of documents, or attend a Tribunal hearing to give evidence or produce documents, where that requirement is imposed by the Tribunal Procedure Rules in relation to an SEN appeal. Under *subsection (6)* a person guilty of such an offence is liable on summary conviction to a fine not exceeding level 3 on the standard scale. Under the Tribunal Procedure Rules nobody may be compelled to give any evidence or produce any document that the person could not be compelled to give or produce on a trial of an action in a court of law.

263. This section replaces, in England, sections 325, 326, 328, 328A, 329and 336(5A) and (6) of, and paragraphs 8 and 11 of Schedule 27 to, the Education Act 1996.

*Section 52: **Right to mediation***

264. This section sets out that local authorities must inform parents and young people, following a decision in relation to an assessment or a plan or after the plan is made, amended or replaced, of their right to mediation about educational, health and social care issues.

265. Mediation is different to an appeal, in that it seeks to resolve matters through agreement between parents/young people and local authorities rather than through a judicial decision. The mediator must be independent, meaning that he or she cannot be an employee of a local authority.

266. The local authority must also inform parents and young people that before making certain appeals to the Tribunal they must obtain a certificate, either following the receipt of information about mediation or following mediation. If the parent wishes to pursue mediation then they must tell the local authority that they intend to do so and what they want to pursue mediation about and, if they want health provision or a particular kind of health provision included in the plan, what that health provision is.

*Section 53: **Mediation: health care issues***

267. This section sets out that where the parent or young person wants to pursue mediation and the mediation issues include health care provision then the local authority must inform the relevant health commissioning body, either the clinical commissioning group or the NHS Commissioning Board, of the mediation issues and of any health care provision that the parent or young person wants. If the parent or young person just wants mediation about health care provision then the responsible commissioning body or bodies must arrange for mediation, ensure that the mediation is conducted by an independent person and participate in the mediation. If the mediation issues include education and/or social care then the local authority must arrange the mediation, ensure it is conducted by an independent person and the local authority and the responsible health commissioning body must participate. An independent person, in this context, is someone who is not employed by a local authority in England or a clinical commissioning group or the NHS Commissioning Board.

*Section 54: **Mediation: educational and social care issues etc***

268. This section ensures that where the mediation does not include health care issues but involves education and/or social care, the local authority must arrange the mediation, make sure that it is conducted by an independent person and participate in the mediation.

*Section 55: **Mediation***

269. When a parent or young person wishes to bring an appeal about the special educational needs element of a plan, they may do so only if an independent mediation adviser has provided them with information about mediation and how it might help. It will be up to the parents or young person to decide whether to go forward to mediation. Where

they decide to do so, they must take part in mediation before they can bring an appeal to the First-tier Tribunal. Where they decide against mediation they will be able to go straight to appeal.

270. The mediation adviser must issue a certificate to the parent or young person if he or she has provided them with information and advice about pursuing mediation and the parent or young person has informed the adviser that they do not wish to pursue mediation about assessments, the drawing up of plans or the special educational element of the EHC plan. The adviser must also issue a certificate if they have provided information and advice, the parent or young person has told them they wish to pursue mediation with the local authority and has participated in mediation. Parents and young people do not have to contact the mediation adviser if they want mediation about the health or social care elements of the plan.

271. Appeals which only concern the name of a school, college or other institution specified in the EHC plan or the type of school, college or institution specified in the EHC plan or the fact that the EHC plan does not name any school, college or other institution can be made without getting mediation information or going to mediation. This is because the parent or young person will already have been able to request a particular school or institution in the further education sector, and had discussions with the local authority about which institution should be named on the EHC plan. Requiring mediation in these circumstances would involve repeating the same discussions. This section gives the Secretary of State regulation-making powers concerning mediation as listed in this section, including about giving notice, imposing time limits, qualifications and experience of mediation advisers and local authority action following mediation.

*Section 56: **Mediation: supplementary***

272. This section gives the Secretary of State the power to make regulations about mediation, about such things as giving notice, imposing time limits and enabling a local authority or commissioning body to take prescribed steps following the conclusion of mediation. It also defines "mediation adviser", and makes clear that the adviser cannot be an employee of a local authority, clinical commissioning group or the NHS Commissioning Board. This section also defines "commissioning body" in relation to mediation.

*Section 57: **Resolution of disagreements***

273. Local authorities must make arrangements for avoiding or resolving disagreements where the parents of a child with special educational needs, or a young person with such needs, do not agree with how the local authority or an education body (listed in *subsection (9)*) with duties under Part 3 of the Act has carried out those duties. It must also make arrangements to avoid or resolve disagreements between the parents of a child or a young person and any school or post-16 institution specifically about the special educational provision made by the institution for that child or young person. The disagreements in this section also cover disagreements between parents or young people on the one hand and the responsible health commissioning bodies on the other about health care provision at the time assessments or re-assessments are being undertaken or EHC plans are being drawn up or reviewed. Disagreement resolution can also cover disagreements between local authorities and their responsible health commissioning bodies.

274. The section does not require either parents or young people on the one hand, or education bodies, local authorities or health commissioning bodies on the other, to participate in resolving disagreements – use of these arrangements is entirely voluntary.

275. Local authorities must appoint someone who is independent to help resolve a disagreement, or prevent it happening in the first place. Employees of a local authority, clinical commissioning group or the NHS Commissioning Board do not meet the criterion of being independent and cannot take on that role.

276. Local authorities must tell various people, including parents and young people, about the arrangements they have put in place to resolve disagreements.

277. This section replaces, in England, section 332B of the Education Act 1996.

Section 58: Appeals and claims by children: pilot schemes

278. This section gives the Secretary of State a power to establish pilot schemes in local authority areas to enable children to make appeals in relation to their special educational needs and to bring disability discrimination claims against schools to the First-tier Tribunal. Currently the Education Act 1996 and the Equality Act 2010 only give parents such a right.

279. The pilots will test whether the right to appeal is something that children would use, the best way to handle these appeals and the cost implications, with a view to extending the right to children across England. The section establishes the things the pilot scheme can cover. These include the age from which a child may appeal and make claims; how mediation before a child's appeal works; and advice, information and advocacy provided to a child. The section stipulates that the power to make an order establishing pilot schemes is repealed after five years (from the date on which the Act receives Royal Assent).

Section 59: Appeals and claims by children: follow-up provision

280. This section provides the Secretary of State with the power to make an order enabling all children in England to bring appeals and make disability discrimination claims to the First-tier Tribunal.

281. The power would be used after pilots have been run. The Secretary of State may not use this power until pilot schemes have been in place for two years.

282. The section establishes what an order made by the Secretary of State can cover and this includes the age from which a child may bring appeals or make disability discrimination claims; about mediation; and advice, information and advocacy provided to a child (mirroring section 58(2)).

Section 60: Equality Act 2010: claims against schools by disabled young people

283. This section amends the Equality Act 2010 so that young people in England who are over compulsory school age and in school can make disability discrimination claims to the First-tier Tribunal themselves. Currently only the parents of disabled young people can make claims to the Tribunal. This mirrors the provision made in section 51 which allows for young people over compulsory school age to make special educational needs appeals to the Tribunal.

284. This section does not affect the rights of parents of young people in Wales to make disability discrimination claims to the Special Educational Needs Tribunal for Wales. Pilots on giving children and young people in Wales the right to make special educational needs appeals and disability discrimination claims to its Tribunal are being conducted with the right being given to all children and young people in Wales following the pilots. The necessary changes to the Equality Act 2010 and the Education Act 1996 will be achieved through an Act of the Assembly.

Special educational provision: functions of local authorities

Section 61: Special educational provision otherwise than in schools, post-16 institutions etc

285. A local authority may arrange for special educational provision to be made for a child or young person otherwise than in a school, college or provider of relevant early years education. But before it can do so it has to be satisfied that it would be inappropriate

for provision to be made in one of those settings and must have consulted the child's parent or the young person.

286. This provision could include, for example, early years provision that is not part of the free early years provision under section 7 of the Childcare Act 2006.

287. This section replaces, in England, section 319 of the Education Act 1996.

Section 62: Special educational provision outside England and Wales

288. This section enables local authorities to arrange special education provision for a child or young person with an EHC plan outside England and Wales in an institution that specialises in providing for special educational needs, and gives them power to pay for, or contribute to, the costs of the child or young person attending such an institution.

289. This section replaces, in England, section 320 of the Education Act 1996.

Section 63: Fees for special educational provision at non-maintained schools and post-16 institutions

290. Where a local authority is responsible for a child or young person with special educational needs, and special educational provision is made for him or her at a school, post-16 institution or provider of relevant early years education, the local authority must pay the fees for the education and training received where the institution is named in the EHC plan. This also applies if there is no EHC plan and the local authority is satisfied the child or young person requires special educational provision and that it is appropriate for them to receive it at the institution in question.

291. Where board and lodging are provided for the child or young person at such a school or college or place where relevant early years education is provided, the local authority must pay those fees if it is satisfied that special educational provision cannot be made there unless board and lodging are provided.

292. This section replaces, in England, section 348 of the Education Act 1996.

Section 64: Supply of goods and services

293. This section gives local authorities the power to supply goods and services to maintained schools, maintained nursery schools, Academies and institutions in the further education sector (further education colleges or sixth form colleges) that are likely to be attended by a person with an EHC plan that the authority is maintaining for the purpose of supporting children and young people with special educational needs. Local authorities may supply goods and services on terms and conditions they see fit (including payment). Local authorities may supply goods and services to other local authorities and other bodies to help them make special educational provision for children receiving relevant early years education. This could cover specialist services to support children with different special educational needs, for example, sensory impairments.

294. This section replaces, in England, section 318 of the Education Act 1996.

Section 65: Access to schools, post-16 institutions and other institutions

295. This section gives local authorities in England the right to have access at any reasonable time to the premises of a school or other institution in England at which education or training is provided to a child or young person with an EHC plan maintained by the local authority in question, for the purpose of monitoring that education or training.

296. The section replaces, in England, and expands the remit of, section 327 of the Education Act 1996. Section 327 only applies to maintained schools which are maintained by another authority and independent schools. This section takes account of the extended

age remit to which the new special educational needs provisions apply and applies to any institution providing the child or young person with education or training in accordance with an EHC plan. Local authorities will, under this section, have access to schools and special post-16 institutions in Wales (but not to general further education institutions in Wales) for the purpose of monitoring the education or training made under an EHC plan.

Special educational provision: functions of governing bodies and others

Section 66: Using best endeavours to secure special educational provision

297. This section requires that the governing bodies, proprietors or management committees of those institutions listed in *subsection (1)* use their best endeavours to secure that the special educational provision that is called for by a pupil or student's special educational needs is made.

298. The section replaces, in England, and expands the remit of section 317(1)(a) of the Education Act 1996. Section 317 applied to the governing bodies of community, foundation or voluntary schools or maintained nursery schools. The new section takes account of the age remit of the new special educational needs provisions and the expansion in the number of Academies by applying the duty to further education institutions, Academy schools and 16 to 19 Academies. The new section also applies to pupil referral units.

Section 67: SEN co-ordinators

299. This section requires governing bodies of maintained mainstream schools, (including Academy schools) and maintained nursery schools to ensure that there is a member of staff designated as Special Educational Needs (SEN) co-ordinator. The SEN Co-ordinator will have responsibility for co-ordinating special educational provision for children and young people with special educational needs in their school. This can include providing advice to other teachers on supporting children with special educational needs and liaising with agencies outside the school such as social care services.

300. The section gives the Secretary of State power to make regulations requiring governing bodies and proprietors to ensure that SEN Co-ordinators have prescribed qualifications and/or experience and conferring other functions on them in relation to SEN co-ordinators.

301. This section replaces, in England, section 317(3A) and (3B) of the Education Act 1996.

Section 68: Informing parents and young people

302. This section, which applies where a child or young person has no EHC plan, requires governing bodies of maintained schools, maintained nursery schools, the management committees of pupil referral units, and the proprietors of Academy schools and Alternative Provision Academies to tell a child's parent, or the young person when special educational provision is being made for the child or young person. This does not need to happen if the child or young person has an EHC plan since parents of children with EHC plans and young people who have EHC plans will already be aware that special educational provision is being made.

303. This section replaces, in England, section 317A of the Education Act 1996 and extends the provision to include young people.

Section 69: SEN information report

304. This section imposes a duty on the governing bodies of maintained schools and maintained nursery schools in England, and proprietors of Academy schools in

England to prepare a report containing "special educational needs information". Special educational needs information is information about the implementation of the governing body's or proprietor's policy for pupils at the school with special educational needs, and information as to the arrangements for the admission of disabled pupils to the school; the steps taken to prevent less favourable treatment of disabled pupils; the facilities provided to assist access to the school by disabled pupils; and the accessibility plan which schools must publish under the Equality Act 2010. Regulations will set out the information to be provided.

305. This section replaces, in England, section 317(5) and (6) of the Education Act 1996. This information is currently published on schools' websites.

Detained Persons

Section 70: Application of Part to detained persons

306. This section sets out which sections of this Part apply to those in custody, namely children and young people that are detained in pursuance of a court order or an order of recall made by the Secretary of State (*subsection (1)*).

307. *Subsection (3)* provides a power for regulations to apply any provision of this Part with or without modifications and *subsection (4)* places a duty on the Secretary of State to consult with the Welsh Ministers before making those regulations if they apply provision under the Part to those detained in Wales.

308. This section defines key terms such as "detained person" (a child or young person under 19 who is detained in a young offender institution, secure training centre or secure children's home), "detained person's EHC needs assessment" and "appropriate person".

309. *Subsection (7)* provides a power for the Secretary of State to make regulations to modify the definition of "the home authority" which is set out in the Education Act 1996. This power might be required for instance where a detained person with an EHC plan is also a looked after child.

Section 71: Assessment of post-detention education, health and care needs of detained persons

310. This section mirrors section 36 and allows the detained young person or a detained child's parent, or the person in charge of the secure accommodation to request an EHC needs assessment. It requires the home local authority to consider whether an assessment is necessary where such a request has been made or where someone else has brought the child or young person to the authority's attention. This section sets out the local authority's duties when making their decision about whether to carry out an assessment and in carrying out any subsequent assessment of the child or young person. In making a decision on whether an assessment is necessary, the local authority must consult with the child's parents or the young person and the person in charge of the secure accommodation in which the child or young person is detained.

311. If the local authority decides not to carry out an assessment they must inform the child's parents or the young person and the person in charge of the secure accommodation in which the child or young person is detained with their reasons for the decision. If they intend to carry out an education, health and care needs assessment they must inform the child's parents or the young person and the person in charge of the secure accommodation in which the child or young person is detained to make sure that they are aware of their rights to have their own views considered by the local authority (either orally or in writing).

312. The local authority must carry out an assessment if, after taking account of any views expressed and evidence submitted, it thinks that the child or young person has or may

have special educational needs and that it may be necessary for special educational provision to be made for them through an EHC plan on their release from detention. The parent or young person and the person in charge of the secure accommodation in which the child or young person is detained should be informed of the outcome of the assessment and whether the local authority intends to prepare an EHC Plan.

313. Regulations may specify how assessments for EHC plans will apply in custody.

Section 72: Securing EHC plans for certain detained persons

314. This section places a duty on the detained person's home local authority to secure an EHC plan if the detained person's EHC needs assessment concludes that one is necessary. Sections 37(2) to (5), 33(2) to (7) and 38 to 40 will apply in relation to an EHC plan secured for a detained person as they would for a child or young person who is not detained.

Section 73: EHC plans for certain detained persons: appeals and mediation

315. This section provides a right of appeal for detained persons. It enables the parents of children and young people to appeal to the First Tier Tribunal about: a decision by their local authority not to secure an EHC needs assessment; a decision not to secure an EHC plan after an assessment; the school or institution named in the plan; or if no school or institution is named in the plan. Regulations may make provision about appeals made to the Tribunal under this section. Section 52(2) to (5) applies when a detained young person or the parent of a detained child appeals under this section.

316. This section also sets out that where the parent or young person wants to make an appeal to the Tribunal and wishes to pursue mediation, the local authority must arrange for mediation, ensure that the mediation is conducted by an independent person and participate in the mediation. If the mediation issues include education and/or social care then the local authority must arrange the mediation, ensure it is conducted by an independent person and the local authority. An independent person, in this context, is someone who is not employed by a local authority in England or a clinical commissioning group or the National Health Service Commissioning Board.

Section 74: Duty to keep EHC plans for detained persons.

317. This section requires home local authorities to keep an EHC plan for a young person while they are detained in relevant youth accommodation. The local authority must arrange appropriate special educational provision and the health services commissioner appropriate health care provision. This is the provision specified in the EHC plan. If it is not practicable to arrange this provision, provision which corresponds as closely as possible to that in the EHC plan must be arranged. Where the provision specified in the EHC plan is no longer appropriate, provision must be arranged which reasonably appears to be appropriate.

Section 75: Supply of goods and services: detained persons

318. This section allows local authorities in England to supply goods and services to any other authority or person making special educational provision for a detained person. This is to help the local authority meet their duties under section 70. The local authority may set the terms and conditions for the supply of the goods and services.

Information to improve well-being of children and young people with SEN

Section 76: Provision and publication of special needs information

319. This section places a duty on the Secretary of State to exercise his or her information-gathering powers to secure special educational needs information about children and young people under 19 from schools and local authorities and the provision made for

them which he thinks would be likely to help in improving the well-being of those children and young people. This must be published annually, in a form chosen by the Secretary of State, and must not include the names of individuals.

320. This section replaces, in England, section 332C of the Education Act 1996. That power has been used to publish a document each year containing a range of information about the numbers of children and young people with special educational needs, their characteristics, including the types of special educational needs, where they are educated and their achievements.

Code of Practice

Section 77: Code of Practice

321. This section requires the Secretary of State to issue a Code of Practice giving guidance to local authorities, the governing bodies, proprietors and management committees of various institutions, and other bodies listed in *subsection (1)* on the exercise of their functions under these provisions. These bodies must have regard to the Code when carrying out those functions, as must those who help them carry out those functions.

322. The First-tier Tribunal must also have regard to any provision in the Code that it considers to be relevant to any question arising out of a special educational needs appeal with which it is dealing.

323. This section also empowers the Secretary of State to revise the Code from time to time, and requires him or her to publish the current version.

324. This section replaces, in England, section 313 of the Education Act 1996 and widens the scope of the bodies who must have regard to the Code from maintained schools, maintained nursery schools and local authorities to include colleges, Academies, pupil referral units and early years education providers.

Section 78: Making and approval of Code

325. This section sets out the procedure for making and approving the Code of Practice. It requires the Secretary of State, when he proposes to issue or revise a Code of Practice, to prepare a draft, consult those he sees fit and consider representations made by them. If he decides to proceed with the draft he must lay a copy before each House of Parliament.

326. In the case of the first draft of the Code, he cannot issue it until it has been approved by both Houses of Parliament. If he later revises the Code, he must not issue it if, within a period of 40 days, the House resolves not to approve the draft.

327. The section replaces section 314 of the Education Act 1996 in relation to England.

Section 79: Review of resolution of disagreements

328. This section requires the Secretary of State and the Lord Chancellor to carry out a review about how effectively disagreements in relation to children and young people with special educational needs are being resolved. The Secretary of State and the Lord Chancellor must prepare a report on the outcome of the review and lay a report before Parliament within three years from the earliest date on which any provision in Part 3 comes into force.

329. Part of the review will involve piloting the ability of the Tribunal to make recommendations about the health and social care elements of EHC plans in accordance with regulations which will be made under section 51(4)(a) and (5).

Supplementary

Section 80: Parents and young people lacking capacity

330. The section enables regulations to modify any statutory provision for the purpose of giving effect to this Part where the parent of a child, or the young person, lacks capacity at the relevant time. Examples of where modifications might be needed include requesting a school or post-16 institution to be named in the EHC plan, and taking part in mediation. "Lacking capacity" has the same meaning as in the Mental Capacity Act 2005. "Relevant time" means the time at which something is required or permitted to be done by or in relation to a child's parent or young person. A representative is a deputy under the Mental Capacity Act, the person who has been given a lasting power of attorney or an attorney in whom an enduring power of attorney has been vested. Where a young person lacking capacity does not have a representative, the reference to young person should be read as the young person's parent (or where that parent also lacks capacity, to that parent's representative).

331. Regulations under the section may give a deputy under the Mental Capacity Act the power to take the relevant decisions, even where this requires the discharge of parental responsibility, which would otherwise not be permitted by that Act.

Section 81: Disapplication of Chapter 1 of Part 4 of EA 1996 in relation to children in England

332. This section provides for Chapter 1 of Part 4 of the Education Act 1996 to cease to apply in relation to children with special educational needs in the area of a local authority in England when these provisions are implemented. It will continue to apply in relation to Wales and children with SEN statements prepared by a local authority in Wales under that Chapter.

Part 4 – Childcare Etc

Section 84: Childminder agencies

333. This section gives effect to Schedule 4, which amends the Childcare Act 2006 ("the CA 2006") to provide for the registration of childminder agencies on the childcare registers maintained by the Chief Inspector. It also provides for the registration of childminders (and others who offer childcare on domestic premises) with those agencies.

334. Currently anyone wishing to offer childcare provision is obliged to register with the Chief Inspector (unless they are exempt). The amendments to Part 3 of the CA 2006 will enable anyone wishing to offer childcare on domestic premises who would otherwise be obliged to apply to register with the Chief Inspector to register instead with a childminder agency (that is an agency which is itself registered on the early years register or the general childcare register). The Schedule also contains consequential amendments.

Schedule 4: Childminder agencies: amendments

335. Schedule 4 makes the amendments necessary to:

- Enable prospective childminders and certain other providers of childcare on domestic premises to apply to register with a childminder agency as an alternative to making an application to the Chief Inspector;
- Provide for childminder agencies, which must be registered on the early years register or Part A of the general childcare register;
- Enable the Chief Inspector to impose conditions on and inspect childminder agencies;

- Enable the Chief Inspector to take enforcement action in respect of unregistered persons who are falsely representing that they are childminder agencies.

336. Part 1 of Schedule 4 amends section 32 of the CA 2006.

337. Section 32 requires the Chief Inspector to maintain two registers: the early years register and the general childcare register. The early years register currently lists anyone who is registered as the provider of childcare for a young child (that is a child from birth up to the first September after the child turns five) for whom registration is compulsory. The general childcare register is split into two parts. Part A currently lists all those providing childcare for children over the age of 5 but under the age of 8 (later years providers) for whom registration is compulsory. Part B lists all childcare providers who are not required to be registered but have done so voluntarily. *Paragraph 2* therefore inserts a new subsection (2)(b) which provides for early years childminder agencies to be registered on the early years register, a new subsection (4)(b) which provides for later years childminder agencies to be registered in Part A of the general childcare register, and amends subsection (5) so that Part B will only list childcare providers registered on the voluntary register by the Chief Inspector.

338. Part 2 of Schedule 4 amends Chapter 2 of the CA 2006 to allow for the registration of childminders and those who offer other early years provision on domestic premises with early years childminder agencies. It also introduces a new Chapter 2A concerning the registration and regulation of early years childminder agencies. Early years childminder agencies will register early years childminders and other early years providers (those offering early years provision on domestic premises) and provide training and support to such providers. Agencies will also be responsible for monitoring providers registered with them and ensuring that the early years provision is of a sufficient standard.

339. Pursuant to section 33(1) of the CA 2006 a person is prohibited from providing early years childminding in England unless registered in the early years register. Early years childminding is early years provision provided on domestic premises for reward where there are no more than three people providing the care or assisting with its provision (see sections 96(4) and (5)). *Paragraph 4* amends section 33 so that anyone registered with an early years childminder agency can also lawfully provide early years childminding.

340. Section 34 sets out the registration requirements for early years providers other than childminders. Currently anyone wishing to offer early years provision on domestic premises which would be childminding but for the fact that the number of people assisting with the provision is greater than three must be registered in the early years register in respect of the premises. *Paragraph 5* amends section 34 so that these providers can be registered with an early years childminder agency in respect of the premises and can therefore also lawfully offer early years provision.

341. *Paragraph 6* amends section 35 so as to allow anyone who proposes to offer early years childminding to make an application for registration to an early years childminder agency or to the Chief Inspector. Subsection (2)(c) is amended so that only applications to the Chief Inspector need to be accompanied by a prescribed fee. Childminder agencies may charge such fees to childminders as they wish, and this will not be prescribed in legislation. *Paragraph 6* also introduces new subsection (4A). It allows a childminder agency to grant an application for registration if a childminder is not disqualified from registration by regulations under section 75 of the CA 2006 and it appears to the agency that the childminder has met the prescribed requirements for registration (and is likely to continue to do so) and any other reasonable requirements that the agency has imposed. "Other reasonable requirements" may include requirements about the qualification levels or experience of childminders. Unlike the Chief Inspector, a childminder agency has discretion as to whether to register a childminder who otherwise meets the prescribed requirements for registration.

342. New subsection (5)(aa) provides that the power to prescribe requirements for registration can be used to prohibit childminders from being registered on both the early years register and with a childminder agency at the same time. New subsection (5)(ab) provides that the power to prescribe requirements for registration can be used to prohibit childminders from being registered with an early years childminder agency as an early years childminder, whilst registered with another childminder agency or by the Chief Inspector in the early years register or general childcare register.

343. *Paragraph 7* introduces a new subsection (1A) into section 36 so as to allow anyone who proposes to offer early years provision on domestic premises which would be childminding but for section 96(5) to make an application for registration either to the Chief Inspector or to a childminder agency in respect of the premises. Once amended, section 36 will operate in the same way as section 35, as amended, which concerns applications for registration by early years childminders.

344. *Paragraph 9* introduces new section 37A which places an obligation on early years childminder agencies to place successful applicants in the register maintained by the agency and to issue them with certificates of registration. It also requires registration certificates to set out particular information as prescribed in regulations and makes provision for amended certificates.

345. *Paragraph 11* amends section 44 of the CA 2006 so that a "relevant instrument" (that is a learning and development order or regulation prescribing welfare requirements made under section 39(1)) may also confer powers and impose duties on early years childminder agencies in the exercise of their functions under Part 3. In particular it may require an early years childminder agency, in exercising these functions, to have regard to factors, standards and other matters prescribed by or referred to in the instrument. It also provides for allegations that a person has failed to have regard to factors, standards and other matters to be taken into account by an agency.

346. *Paragraph 12* amends section 49 of the CA 2006 so that provisions relating to inspection apply only to childminders or other early years providers registered on the early years register. New section 51D in *paragraph 13* makes provision for inspections of childminder agencies. Childminders registered with early years childminder agencies will not be subject to inspections under section 49. Instead, it is intended that they will be subject to regular monitoring visits from the agency they are registered with, where the agency will assess and report on the standards of care being delivered (including how well the childminder meets the requirements of the Early Years Foundation Stage). Inspections of early years childminder agencies under new section 51D also allow for the Chief Inspector to inspect early years providers registered with an agency as part of the agency's inspection.

347. *Paragraph 13* of the Schedule inserts a new Chapter 2A into Part 3 of the CA 2006 comprising new sections 51A to 51F relating to the registration and regulation of early years childminder agencies. These sections are similar in effect to the equivalent sections relating to the registration by the Chief Inspector of childcare providers.

348. Section 51A deals with applications for registration by early years childminder agencies. Subsection (3) requires the Chief Inspector to grant an application for registration as an early years childminder agency if the applicant is not disqualified from registration and the requirements for registration, which will be set out in regulations, are satisfied and are likely to continue to be satisfied. Subsection (4) requires the Chief Inspector to refuse an application where the applicant is disqualified and/or where the requirements set out in regulations are not met.

349. Subsection (5) sets out some of the matters which the regulations may deal with and these include (but are not limited to) requirements relating to the applicant, the agency's arrangements for registering early years providers and the provision, to the Chief Inspector, of information about early years providers registered with the applicant. Subsection (5)(f) allows for requirements in relation to the agency's arrangements for

training and monitoring early years providers and providing them with information, advice and assistance. Subsection (5)(g) allows for requirements in relation to the agency's arrangements for ensuring that early years provision (of those registered with it) is of a sufficient standard.

350. Section 51B places an obligation on the Chief Inspector to place successful applicants in the early years register and to issue them with certificates of registration. It also requires registration certificates to set out particular information as prescribed in regulations and makes provision for amended certificates.

351. Section 51C deals with conditions on registration for early years childminder agencies. It allows the Chief Inspector to impose any appropriate conditions at any time and to vary or remove any conditions at any time. Under subsection (4) it is an offence if, without reasonable excuse, a person does not comply with registration conditions.

352. Section 51D relates to inspection of early years childminder agencies. It requires the Chief Inspector to inspect early years childminder agencies at the request of the Secretary of State. It also allows the Chief Inspector to inspect early years childminder agencies at any other time when the Chief Inspector considers it appropriate. Subsection (2) allows the Chief Inspector, as part of an agency's inspection, to inspect the early years provision provided by those registered with the agency to ensure that the Chief Inspector is able to assess the quality of support being offered by the agency through visiting providers registered with an agency. Subsection (3) allows the Chief Inspector to charge a fee, as prescribed in regulations, for an inspection of an early years childminder agency, when both the agency has requested an inspection and the Secretary of State requires it. This mirrors section 85, which enables the Chief Inspector to charge a fee if he carries out an inspection of an early years provider at the request of the provider. Subsection (4) provides for regulations to require the early years childminder agency to notify particular people of an inspection. Regulations could, for example, require agencies to notify childminders registered with them of an impending inspection.

353. Section 51E sets out requirements for the Chief Inspector to report, in writing, following an inspection of an early years childminder agency and makes provision for the distribution of copies of the report. Subsection (3) allows for regulations to be made requiring the agency to make copies of the report available to prescribed persons. This could include, for example, childminders registered with the agency and parents who place their children in the care of childminders registered with that agency.

354. Section 51F makes it an offence for a person to falsely represent that they are an early years childminder agency. This would mean, for example, that a person purporting to register childminders and other early years providers who was not registered as an agency on the early years register would be committing an offence.

355. Part 3 of Schedule 4 (later years childminder agencies) amends Chapter 3 of the CA 2006 to allow for the registration of childminders and others who offer later years provision on domestic premises for children under eight with later years childminder agencies. It also introduces a new Chapter 3A concerning the regulation of later years childminder agencies. Later years childminder agencies will register later years childminders and other later years providers (those offering later years provision on domestic premises) who would otherwise be required to register in Part A of the general childcare register and provide training and support to such providers. Agencies will also be responsible for monitoring providers registered with them.

356. Later years provision in relation to a child means the provision of childcare at any time from the first September following his/her 5th birthday up to the age of 18 (see section 96(6)). Later years childminding is later years provision provided on domestic premises for reward where there are no more than three people providing the care or assisting with its provision (see sections 96(8) and (9)). Pursuant to section 52(1), a person cannot provide later years childminding for a child under the age of eight

unless registered on Part A of the general childcare register maintained by the Chief Inspector. *Paragraph 15* amends section 52 so that anyone registered with a later years childminder agency can also lawfully provide later years childminding. Similarly, *paragraph 16* amends section 53 so that others offering later years provision on domestic premises for a child under the age of eight can be registered with a later years childminder agency in respect of the premises and can therefore also lawfully offer later years provision.

357. *Paragraphs 17* to *23* make amendments to the provisions of the CA 2006 which deal with the process of registration for later years childminders and other later years providers on domestic premises. The amendments provide for the possibility of registration with later years childminder agencies. The registration process will mirror that which applies to early years childminders and other early years providers who seek to register with an early years childminder agency, as described above by reference to *paragraphs 6 to 10* of Schedule 4.

358. *Paragraph 22* introduces a new section 57A into the CA 2006. It requires a childminder agency which is both an early years and later years agency, on request, to register a person as a later years provider where that person is already registered with the agency as an early years provider.

359. *Paragraph 24* amends section 59 of the CA 2006. This is the later years equivalent to section 44 of the CA 2006. This section allows the Secretary of State to make regulations governing the activities of registered later years providers. These may cover issues such as the welfare of children, suitability of persons and premises, complaints procedures and the provision of information. Subsections (4) and (5) have been amended so as to allow regulations to confer powers or impose duties on later years childminder agencies, in particular the need to have regard to standards and other matters prescribed in the regulations. Subsection (6) has been amended to provide for allegations that a person has failed to have regard to factors, standards and other matters to be taken into account by an agency.

360. *Paragraph 25* amends section 60 of the CA 2006 so that provisions relating to inspection apply only to childminders or other later years providers registered in Part A of the general childcare register. New section 61E makes provision for inspections of later years childminder agencies. Childminders registered with later years childminder agencies will not be subject to inspections under section 60. Instead, it is intended that they will be subject to regular monitoring visits from the agency they are registered with, where the agency will assess and report on the standards of care being delivered. New section 61E also allows for the Chief Inspector to inspect later years providers registered with an agency as part of the agency's inspection.

361. *Paragraph 26* of the Schedule inserts a new Chapter 3A into Part 3 of the CA 2006, comprising new sections 61A to 61G, relating to the registration and regulation of later years childminder agencies.

362. The process of registration for later years childminder agencies and the Chief Inspector's powers and obligations in respect of the registration and inspection of later years childminder agencies mirror those for early years childminder agencies. A special procedure has, however, been introduced for early years childminder agencies who notify the Chief Inspector that they wish to operate as a later years childminder agency. Section 61C requires the Chief Inspector, on request, to register a person in Part A of the general childcare register if that person is already registered in the early years register as an early years childminder agency. This means that an agency need not go through the registration process twice.

363. Part 4 of Schedule 4 includes provisions to enable those already registered with a childminder agency in respect of early or later years provision to register provision that is otherwise exempt from registration at the same agency on a voluntary basis. Provision exempt from registration includes, for example, later years childminding for

a child who has attained the age of eight, or early years or later years childminding in respect of which the person is not required to be registered under Chapter 2 or 3 of the CA 2006. Part 4 introduces new section 65A into the CA 2006, which provides for a simplified application process for those already registered with a childminder agency who wish to register in respect of provision that is otherwise exempt from registration. Section 67 is also amended to enable the Secretary of State to exercise his or her power to make regulations governing activities of persons who register voluntarily so as to impose duties or confer powers on childminder agencies as well as the Chief Inspector.

364. Part 5 of Schedule 4 includes provisions which apply to all childminder agencies. It includes provisions relating to cancellation and suspension of registration, disqualification from registration and removal from the registers. It also includes provisions dealing with the Chief Inspector's powers of entry, and powers and duties in relation to provision of information about providers. Provision is made relating to offences and criminal proceedings.

365. *Paragraph 33* amends section 68 (cancellation of registration) so that this section only applies to childcare providers who are registered on the early years or general childcare register. The cancellation of registration for persons registered with childminder agencies will be dealt with in regulations made under new section 69A. New section 69B deals with the cancellation of a childminder agency's registration.

366. *Paragraph 34* amends section 69 (suspension of registration) so that it only applies to childcare providers on the early years or general childcare register. The suspension of registration for those registered with childminder agencies will also be dealt with in regulations made under new section 69A. New section 69C deals with the suspension of a childminder agency's registration.

367. *Paragraph 35* introduces new section 69A which allows for the making of regulations dealing with the cancellation, termination and suspension of a provider's registration with a childminder agency. In particular, regulations may make provision for situations when a provider voluntarily terminates their registration with an agency. It also allows for offences to be created relating to things done while a person's registration with an agency is suspended. Regulations may also make provision concerning how disputes are to be resolved between agencies and providers registered with them.

368. Section 69B deals with cancellation of the registration of a childminder agency registered on a childcare register. It requires the Chief Inspector to cancel registration if a person becomes disqualified from registration and allows the Chief Inspector to cancel registration where prescribed requirements for registration are not met, conditions of registration are not complied with or fees are not paid. Subsection (4) enables regulations to make provisions about the effect of cancellation of an agency's registration on the providers registered with that agency. Regulations may, for example, enable providers to be provisionally registered with the Chief Inspector in these circumstances so that they are able to continue to provide childcare as registered providers while they seek alternative registration with the Chief Inspector or another childminder agency.

369. Section 69C enables the Secretary of State to make regulations allowing a person's registration as a childminder agency to be suspended for a particular period in certain circumstances. Where a childminder agency has its registration suspended, it must not carry out any functions of a childminder agency or represent that it is able to do so. Otherwise the agency will be committing an offence (see subsection (6)). Subsection (3) allows regulations to make provisions about the effect of an agency's suspension on the providers registered with that agency.

370. *Paragraph 38* introduces new section 70A which allows childminder agencies to give notice to the Chief Inspector when they wish to be removed from either of the registers. The Chief Inspector must remove from the register any agency which has given notice. However, the Chief Inspector may not remove the person if the Chief Inspector has

already sent notice of intention to cancel registration and has not yet decided against that step or has already sent notice of a decision to cancel registration and the time for appeal is still running.

371. Section 72 enables the Chief Inspector to apply to a Justice of the Peace for an order cancelling registration, varying or removing a registration condition or imposing a new condition.*Paragraph 40* amends section 72 so that the Chief Inspector can only make such an application in relation to providers on the early years or general childcare register. Such an application cannot be sought by, or made in relation to, a childminder agency, or a childminder registered with a childminder agency. Regulations under section 69A will set out the requirements for childminder agencies in terms of dealing with providers' registrations in situations where it appears that children in the care of those providers may be suffering or are likely to suffer significant harm. There is no equivalent provision for cancellation of registration or the imposition of conditions on childminder agencies in an emergency as they will not be directly caring for children.

372. *Paragraphs 43* and *44* make amendments to reflect that section 75 (disqualification from registration) applies only to early years and later years providers and not to childminder agencies (who are covered by the disqualification provisions in new section 76A).

373. *Paragraph 45* introduces new subsections (3A) to (3C) into section 76 which provide that an early years or later years childminder agency must not register any person who is disqualified from registration under regulations made pursuant to section 75. Contravention of these prohibitions is an offence under subsection (4) although these are subject to the defence at new subsection (6A).

374. *Paragraph 46* introduces new sections 76A and 76B. New section 76A is largely based on section 75 of the CA 2006. It provides for the Secretary of State to make regulations setting out when a person may be disqualified from registration as a childminder agency. Subsection (3) enables regulations to be made allowing the Chief Inspector to waive disqualification in certain circumstances.

375. Section 76B sets out the consequences of disqualification for childminder agencies. These are that a disqualified person must not exercise any functions of a childminder agency, purport to exercise such functions, or be a member of the governing body, director, manager or other officer of, or partner in, an agency or otherwise be directly concerned in the management of an agency. A disqualified person is also prevented from working for an agency in a capacity which involves entering premises on which early or later years provision is being provided. Subsection (2) prevents an agency from employing a disqualified person in any capacity which involves direct concern in the management of that agency or entering childcare premises. Contravention of these prohibitions is an offence.

376. *Paragraph 47* amends section 77 (which concerns the Chief Inspector's powers of entry) so that it applies only in relation to early and later years providers. Entry to the premises of childminder agencies is dealt with in new section 78A. Subsection (2) of section 77 is amended so that the Chief Inspector may enter the premises of a provider registered with a childminder agency for the purposes of conducting an inspection of the agency.

377. *Paragraph 49* inserts new section 78A to give a person authorised by the Chief Inspector the power of entry, at any reasonable time, in respect of any premises in England if he has reasonable cause to believe that a person on the premises is falsely representing that it is an early years or later years childminder agency. It also gives a power of entry in respect of the premises of any childminder agency at any reasonable time (subsection (2)) for the purposes described in subsection (3), which are to conduct an inspection under section 51E or 61F, and to determine if conditions on, or requirements for, registration are being met. Under subsection (8) it is an offence

intentionally to obstruct a person exercising powers under this section. Subsection (9) specifies the penalty for the offence, a fine not exceeding level 4 on the standard scale.

378. New section 78B deals with circumstances in which a power of entry conferred by section 78A is exercisable on domestic premises. In the case of agencies, this would be where an agency's registered address is also domestic premises. If the premises are the home of someone who is not employed by the childminder agency, or a member, manager, director or other officer of the agency, section 78B requires the consent of an adult occupying the property before a power of entry under the Act may be exercised (see subsection (2)).

379. *Paragraph 51* amends section 82 of the CA 2006 to allow the Chief Inspector to require from a childminder agency information about their activities as an agency. The information is limited to that which the Chief Inspector considers it is necessary to have for the purpose of his or her functions under Part 3. Subsection (2) provides that this power includes a power for the Chief Inspector to require an early years or later years childminder agency to provide him or her with information about an early years or later years provider registered with the agency.

380. *Paragraph 53* introduces new section 83A to require childminder agencies to give the Secretary of State, HMRC and the relevant local authority information (to be prescribed in regulations) when it takes certain steps under Part 3, such as registering a childcare provider. The information which may be prescribed is, in the case of the Secretary of State, information that the Sectary of State may require for the purposes of functions in relation to universal credit under Part 1 of the Welfare Reform Act 2012, in the case of HMRC, information relevant to their functions relating to tax credits and, in the case of local authorities, information which would assist them in the running of the information service which they are required to establish under section 12 of the CA 2006.

381. *Paragraph 55* inserts new section 84A to allow childminder agencies to make prescribed information about registered persons available (to such persons and in such manner as they feel appropriate) for the purposes of assisting parents in choosing a childcare provider and protecting children from harm and neglect. Subsection (3) enables the Secretary of State to make regulations requiring childminder agencies to provide prescribed information about registered persons to prescribed people for either of those purposes. This could include, for example, passing information to the police or other child protection agencies for the purpose of protecting children from harm.

382. *Paragraph 58* amends section 89 so that regulations concerning fees payable to the Chief Inspector relating to the exercise of his or her functions under Part 3 apply only to those on the early years or general childcare registers (that is, childminder agencies and childcare providers registered by the Chief Inspector). Fees for providers registering with childminder agencies will not be prescribed and agencies will be able to set their own fees in respect of the services they will provide.

383. For the purpose of making decisions about registration, it may be necessary for the Chief Inspector to obtain information from third parties which relates to an applicant for registration or a registered person (or from other persons who may be caring for the children concerned). Section 90 enables the Secretary of State to make regulations allowing the Chief Inspector to refuse or to cancel registration if consent from the person whom the information concerns to the disclosure of that information by third parties is withheld or consent is withdrawn. *Paragraph 59* extends section 90 so as to encompass the registration of childminder agencies.

384. Section 98 of the CA 2006 is amended by *paragraph 62* to provide a definition of "childminder agency", "early years childminder agency" and "later years childminder agency." New subsection (1A) is inserted so as to make clear that a person is registered for the purposes of Part 3 of the Act if they are registered on either of the early years or general childcare registers or they are registered with an early years or later years childminder agency.

385. Part 6 of the Schedule (other amendments) includes, at *paragraph 63*, an amendment to section 99. Section 99(1) allows regulations to make provision requiring all registered early years providers, and school-based providers who are exempted from registration requirements by section 34(2), to provide "individual child information" (as defined in that section) to the Secretary of State or any prescribed person. *Paragraph 63* extends that provision to ensure that early years childminder agencies can also be required, by regulations, to provide certain individual child information to prescribed persons.

386. *Paragraph 64* makes an amendment to the Employment Agencies Act 1973 so that childminder agencies are exempted from that Act. As childminder agencies will be subject to regulation by the Chief Inspector, and by regulations made under the CA 2006, this exemption also means that they are not subjected to a further regulatory regime.

Section 85: ***Inspection of providers of childcare to young children***

387. This section amends section 49 of the CA 2006, which relates to the inspection of early years childcare provision. It enables the Chief Inspector to charge a fee for an inspection that is carried out at the request of the provider, where that inspection is also required by the Secretary of State. Equivalent provision enabling the Chief Inspector to charge a fee for the re-inspection of childminder agencies is made by *paragraphs 13* and *26* of Schedule 4, which introduce new sections 51D(3) and 61E(3) respectively.

Section 86: ***Repeal of local authority's duty to assess sufficiency of childcare provision***

388. This section repeals the duty in section 11 of the CA 2006 on English local authorities to prepare, at least every three years, an assessment of the sufficiency of the provision of childcare in their area.

Section 87: ***Discharge of authority's duty to secure free early years provision***

389. This section makes provision for regulations to be made about the discharge of the duty on local authorities to secure free early years provision for young children. Under such regulations, a requirement is imposed on local authorities to meet this duty by securing early years provision at any provider which meets the description in regulations, which meets the terms of funding, and where a parent of an eligible child wishes to send that child. Regulations may also be made specifying the conditions local authorities may and may not attach to the arrangements they make to discharge this duty.

Section 88: ***Governing bodies: provision of community facilities***

390. This section removes the requirements in section 28(4) and (5) of the Education Act 2002 for maintained schools in England (it preserves the effect of the section in respect of Wales).

391. Section 27 of the Education Act 2002 gives the governing bodies of maintained schools the power to make available facilities or services of the school for the benefit of the school's pupils and their families, and the people who live or work locally. These services might take the form of childcare before or after the school day, for example. Previously, if maintained schools wanted to make this kind of provision, section 28(4) of the Education Act 2002 required their governing bodies to consult with their local authority, their staff, and the parents of pupils registered at the school. In addition, section 28(5) of the Education Act 2002 required the governing bodies of maintained schools in England to have regard to advice or guidance from the Secretary of State or their local authority when offering this type of provision.

Section 89: Childcare costs scheme: preparatory expenditure

392. This section enables HMRC to incur expenditure in preparing for the introduction of a scheme for providing assistance in respect of the costs of childcare.

393. The Government has announced that it intends to introduce a new tax-free childcare scheme to assist working families in meeting the costs of formal childcare. Further legislation will be introduced as required setting out the details of the scheme.

PART 5 – WELFARE OF CHILDREN

Section 90: Extension of licensing of child performances to children under 14

394. This section repeals section 38 of the Children and Young Persons Act 1963 in relation to England and Wales. The effect of that repeal is to remove restrictions on the circumstances in which a local authority can issue a performance licence to a child under the age of 14.

Section 91: Purchase of tobacco etc. on behalf of persons under 18

395. This section introduces an offence in England and Wales of "proxy purchasing" of tobacco products and cigarette papers. This makes it an offence for a person aged 18 or over to buy, or attempt to buy, tobacco or cigarette papers on behalf of a person under the age of 18. If found guilty of an offence, the penalty is a fine not exceeding level 4 on the standard scale. This section also provides local authority enforcement officers with the flexibility to issue fixed penalty notices if they believe an offence has been committed. To enable effective enforcement, the section provides enforcement officers with powers of entry.

396. These provisions apply to England and Wales.

Section 92: Prohibition of sale of nicotine products to persons under 18

397. This section provides the Secretary of State with the power to make regulations to prohibit the sale of nicotine products to persons under the age of 18.

398. Subsections (9) to (11) explain what is meant by nicotine products. Examples of nicotine products include an electronic cigarette and part of an electronic cigarette. Tobacco products, which are already subject to a prohibition on sale to persons aged under 18, are not nicotine products for the purposes of this section. The powers at subsection (7) enable the Secretary of State to provide for exceptions or to make provision in relation to nicotine products of a specified kind or all nicotine products.

399. There is an exemption for under 18s employed in the industry and a due diligence defence. The penalty for committing the offence is a fine not exceeding level 4 on the standard scale. These provisions apply to England and Wales.

400. Regulations made under these powers will be subject to the affirmative parliamentary procedure and the Secretary of State must obtain the consent of the Welsh Ministers before making regulations under this section which would be within the legislative competence of the National Assembly for Wales.

Section 93: Amendments consequential on section 92

401. This section makes consequential amendments to integrate the new age of sale offence for nicotine products into the existing age of sale legislation for tobacco products. Consequential amendments to section 5 of the Children and Young Persons (Protection from Tobacco) Act 1991 apply the enforcement regime for tobacco age of sale offences to an offence under section 92. Consequential amendments to sections 12A to 12D of the Children and Young Persons Act 1933 integrate the offence under section 92 into the existing regime for repeated tobacco age of sale offences.

*Section 94: **Regulation of retail packaging etc of tobacco products***

402. This section gives the Secretary of State the power to make regulations about specified elements of the retail packaging of tobacco products and the products themselves where he or she considers that the regulations may contribute to reducing the risk of harm to, or to promoting, the health or welfare of children.

403. These provisions apply to the whole of the UK. Regulations made under these powers will be subject to the affirmative parliamentary procedure and the Secretary of State must obtain the consent of the Scottish Ministers, Welsh Ministers, or Office of the First Minister or Deputy First Minister of Northern Ireland, where they contain provisions which would be within the legislative competence of their respective Parliament or Assembly.

*Section 95: **Smoking in a private vehicle***

404. This section amends smoke-free legislation (the Health Act 2006) to provide the Secretary of State, or Welsh Ministers in relation to Wales, with the power to make regulations to provide for a private vehicle to be smoke-free when a person under the age of 18 is present in the vehicle. The Health Act 2006 contains two offences in relation to vehicles that are designated as smoke-free under the regulations: smoking in a smoke-free vehicle and failure by the person in control of the vehicle to prevent smoking in a smoke-free vehicle.

405. The Health Act 2006 includes a power to provide for penalty notices in relation to the offence of smoking in a smoke-free vehicle and this section amends that Act to allow penalty notices to also be used for the offence of failing to prevent smoking in a vehicle when a person under the age of 18 is present.

406. All regulations made under these powers will be subject to the affirmative parliamentary procedure.

*Section 96: **Young carers***

407. This section consolidates existing rights for young carers, in particular from the Carers (Recognition and Services) Act 1995 and the Carers and Disabled Children Act 2000, and insert new sections into Part 3 of the Children Act 1989.

408. This section also extends the right to an assessment of needs for support to all young carers under the age of 18 regardless of who they care for, what type of care they provide or how often they provide it. It requires a local authority to carry out an assessment of a young carer's needs for support on request or on the appearance of need, and provides for local authorities to combine the assessment of a young carer with an assessment of the person they care for. Previously, a young carer had to request such an assessment. The section enables the Secretary of State to make regulations making provision about the carrying out of a young carer's needs assessment. Those regulations may, in particular, specify matters to which a local authority is to have regard or is to determine in carrying out the assessment, the manner in which an assessment is to be carried out and the form that assessment is to take.

*Section 97: **Parent carers***

409. This section consolidates into Part 3 of the Children Act 1989 existing legislation, in particular the Carers and Disabled Children Act 2000, which gives individuals with parental responsibility for a disabled child the right to an assessment of their needs by a local authority. This consolidation simplifies the legislation relating to parent carers of disabled children, making rights and duties clearer to both parent and practitioners. It removes the requirement for such carers to be providing "a substantial amount of care on a regular basis" in order to be assessed, and requires local authorities to assess on the appearance of need, as well as on request.

410. This section requires local authorities explicitly to have regard to the well-being of parent carers in undertaking an assessment of their needs. The definition of well-being will be the same as in Part 1 of the Care Act 2014 (subject to Parliamentary approval of the Care Act).

411. This section enables the Secretary of State to make regulations making provision about the carrying out of a parent carer's needs assessment. Those regulations may, in particular, specify matters to which a local authority is to have regard or is to determine in carrying out the assessment, the manner in which an assessment is to be carried out and the form that assessment is to take.

Section 98: ***Arrangements for living with former foster parents after reaching adulthood***

412. This section inserts a new section 23CZA into the Children Act 1989. New section 23CZA sets out what constitutes a staying put arrangement, the duties placed on local authorities for the duration of the arrangement and the conditions that underpin the support from the local authority. Section 23CZA(2) provides that a staying put arrangement is one where the young person is someone who was in care immediately prior to their 18th birthday as an eligible child, and that person continues to reside with their former foster carer once they turn 18.

413. So long as the arrangement is consistent with the welfare of the young person, the local authority is required to provide advice, assistance and support to them and their former foster parent to support the maintenance of the arrangement. The local authority is also required to monitor the arrangement (section 23CZA(3)).

414. The support provided to the former foster carer must include financial support (section 23CZA(4)).

415. *Subsection (3)* inserts a new paragraph 19BA into Schedule 2 to the Children Act 1989 which places a duty on local authorities to determine once the child becomes an eligible child, the appropriateness of working towards facilitating a future staying put arrangement.

416. These duties will continue until the young person reaches the age of 21 unless either they or their former foster parent decides to end the arrangement sooner.

Section 99: ***Promotion of educational achievement of children looked after by local authorities***

417. Section 22 of the Children Act 1989 places a general duty on local authorities to safeguard and promote the welfare of the children they look after. Section 22(3A) places a particular duty on local authorities in England to promote the educational achievement of the children they look after, regardless of where they are placed. Many local authorities in England have an education lead to champion the needs of looked after children. They are often referred to as "Virtual School Heads" (VSH), because they monitor and track the educational progress of the children looked after by their authority as if they attended a single school.

418. This section amends section 22 by inserting new subsections (3B) and (3C). Subsection (3B) requires every local authority in England to appoint an officer employed by the authority to make sure the duty under section 22(3A) is properly discharged. Subsection (3C) requires that the person appointed under subsection (3B) is an officer employed by that local authority or another local authority in England.

419. The section makes explicit reference to permitting a local authority to appoint more than one officer to perform this role.

420. There is existing statutory guidance from the Department for Education, issued under section 7 of the Local Authority Social Services Act 1970, about how local authorities

should discharge their duty to promote the education of their looked after children. This guidance will be revised to take account of this new provision. The revised guidance will also explain the relationship between the functions of the appointed officer carrying out the role of the Virtual School Head and the Director of Children's Services ("DCS"). In effect, the DCS, who is appointed for the purposes of the authority's social services functions relating to children, is responsible for promoting the educational achievement of the children looked after by the authority. The appointed officer or VSH and the service he or she manages will be responsible for how this is achieved.

Section 100: ***Duty to support pupils with medical conditions***

421. This section places a duty on governing bodies of maintained schools, proprietors of Academies and management committees of pupil referral units to make arrangements for supporting pupils at school with medical conditions. In meeting that duty, the section requires all of those bodies to have regard to guidance issued by the Secretary of State under this provision.

Section 101: ***Local authority functions relating to children etc: intervention***

422. This section clarifies the law in relation to the Secretary of State's power to intervene under section 497A(4A) of the Education Act 1996 and section 50 of the Children Act 2004, where a local authority is failing to deliver services to an adequate standard. The section ensures that these powers would be exercised effectively, in particular in the interests of certainty for children who may be taken into care or placed for adoption.

423. Parallel amendments are also made to the Secretary of State's power to intervene under section 15 of the Local Government Act 1999 where he or she is satisfied that a best value authority is failing to comply with the requirements of Part 1 of that Act.

424. *Subsection (2)* amends section 497A of the Education Act 1996 to clarify the effect of the power in section 497A(4A) of that Act. This puts beyond doubt that either the Secretary of State or a nominee, exercising functions in place of a local authority pursuant to a direction under section 497A(4A) of the Education Act 1996 can, for example, apply for or be named in care orders under section 31 of the Children Act 1989, exercise the adoption related functions set out in section 92(2) of the Adoption and Children Act 2002 and exercise certain other court-related functions in the same way as a local authority. The section makes it clear that, following such a direction, other relevant references in legislation to a "local authority", such as in relation to the Chief Inspector's functions and powers under sections 136 to 141 of the Education and Inspections Act 2006, are to be read as references to the Secretary of State or a nominee.

425. *Subsection (3)* amends section 15 of the Local Government Act 1999 to clarify the effect of the power in section 15(6) of that Act. This clarifies the Secretary of State's intervention powers under that Act in the same way as *subsection (2)* does in relation to the Secretary of State's power in section 497A(4A) of the Education Act 1996.

Section 102: ***Application of suspension etc powers to establishments and agencies in England***

426. This section makes available to the Chief Inspector the powers in sections 14A and 20B of the Care Standards Act 2000 to suspend a person's registration in respect of an establishment or agency in England. At present these powers are only available to Welsh Ministers in respect of establishments or agencies in Wales. If a registered person continued to operate a setting whilst suspended, they would commit a criminal offence. This section clarifies the Chief Inspector's enforcement powers so action can be taken if, for example, it has serious concerns about the safety and care provided by a regulated setting, such as a children's home, that require an urgent response.

Section 103: Objectives and standards for establishments and agencies in England

427. This section adds a new subsection (1A) into section 22 of the Care Standards Act 2000. It provides for the Secretary of State to have a power to make regulations to prescribe objectives and standards that must be met by an establishment or agency that is regulated by the Chief Inspector. This includes children's homes.

Section 104: National minimum standards for establishments and agencies in England

428. This section amends section 23 of the Care Standards Act 2000, which is concerned with "national minimum standards" (NMS). The section inserts a new section (1A) into section 23 of the Care Standards Act 2000. It provides that the NMS applicable to an establishment or agency regulated by the Chief Inspector, such as a children's home, may explain and supplement regulations made under section 22 of the Care Standards Act 2000.

Section 105: Disqualification from carrying on, or being employed in, a children's home

429. This section amends section 65 of the Children Act 1989, which provides for persons who are disqualified from private fostering under section 68 of that Act to be disqualified from carrying on, managing or having a financial interest in children's homes. This section introduces, in relation to England, a time limit for a person to disclose to the Chief Inspector that they have been disqualified from private fostering.

Section 106: Provision of free school lunches

430. This section amends Part 9 of the Education Act 1996 in relation to the provision of school lunches. It ensures that all state-funded schools – both maintained schools and Academies – have an obligation to provide free school lunches on request for all pupils in infant classes (i.e reception, year one and year two). It also creates an enabling power for the Secretary of State to extend this obligation to other school year groups or to children in maintained nursery schools and other state-funded early years settings.

431. For maintained schools, this new obligation will sit alongside the existing statutory obligations imposed on them in respect of the provision of school lunches. For Academies, the section inserts a new provision requiring all future Academies (where funding agreements are entered into after this amendment comes into effect) to have a provision in their funding agreement that mirrors the school lunch obligations placed on maintained schools; and all funding agreements entered into before this section comes into effect must be read as if they included this requirement.

Part 6 - the Children's Commissioner

Section 107: Primary function of the Children's Commissioner

432. Section 107 replaces section 2 of the Children Act 2004 ("the 2004 Act") with new sections 2 to 2C, and changes the primary function of the Commissioner from one of "promoting awareness of the views and interests of children in England" to one of "promoting and protecting the rights of children in England". The Commissioner's remit also covers non-devolved matters in Scotland, Wales and Northern Ireland as set out in *paragraph 3* of Schedule 5.

433. The role of promoting children's rights entails raising awareness of children's rights and how they should be applied.

434. The role of protecting children's rights should, in practice, mean that the Commissioner is able to challenge any policy or practice which he or she considers may lead, or has led, to an infringement or abuse of children's rights, and provide evidence of any negative

impact of those policies and practices on children's rights to those who are responsible and have sufficient standing to bring about change. The Commissioner does not have the power to require a change to that policy or practice.

435. Promoting awareness of children's views and interests continues to form part of the primary function, as it remains important that children's views inform any comments or recommendations that the Commissioner makes. Section 2(2) achieves this by providing that the function of promoting awareness of the views and interests of children is an aspect of the primary function of promoting and protecting children's rights.

436. Section 2(3) lists some of the activities that the Commissioner may undertake in exercising the primary function. The list is not exhaustive and therefore does not place a limit on the activities the Commissioner may undertake. Many of the activities listed are carried forward from the previous legislation and updated to reflect the new primary function:

- Paragraph (a) concerns the provision of advice to relevant persons on how to act compatibly with children's rights. This aspect of the primary function is likely to involve making recommendations to change policies or practices that the Commissioner considers have infringed or may infringe children's rights;
- Paragraph (b) sets out that the Commissioner may also encourage relevant persons to take account of children's views and interests. This aspect of the Commissioner's role could include providing both general guidance on how best to involve children in the decision-making processes of organisations; and highlighting specific examples of points children have raised in the course of a particular investigation that the Commissioner has undertaken;
- Paragraph (c) carries forward a similar provision from the 2004 Act and extends it to cover "rights" (as well as views and interests) to reflect the change to the Commissioner's primary function;
- Paragraph (d) makes clear that in the discharge of the primary function, the Commissioner can assess the potential impact that proposed new policies or legislation may have on children's rights. It will be for the Commissioner to determine whether to carry out such assessments and on which issues;
- Paragraph (e) makes it clear that the Commissioner may, in particular, bring any matter to the attention of Parliament. Relevant matters could be raised, for example, through the Commissioner's annual report to Parliament or by writing to the chair of a relevant Select Committee;
- Paragraphs (f), (g) and (h) reflect similar provisions in the 2004 Act. In each provision, the words "consider or research" have been replaced with "investigate". In addition, paragraph (g) contains a new provision, linked to paragraph (f), that concerns investigations of the availability and effectiveness (rather than "operation") of advocacy services for children. In carrying out these activities, the Commissioner will want to be satisfied that there is adequate provision in place, and that services are easily accessible, and respond effectively to the issues raised by children;
- Paragraph (h) broadly replicates a provision from the 2004 Act, clarifying that the Commissioner has wide discretion over other matters that he or she chooses to investigate, but provides for this to cover the rights (as well as the interests of) children – to reflect the change to the Commissioner's primary function;
- Paragraph (i) makes clear that the Commissioner's primary function of promoting and protecting rights may include reporting on the implementation of the United Nations Convention on the Rights of the Child (UNCRC) in England (and, under sections 5 to 7, in Wales, Scotland and Northern Ireland, as regards non-devolved

matters). Formal reporting to the UN Committee remains the responsibility of the State Party, but this provision makes it clear that the Commissioner may carry out his or her own independent assessments;

- Paragraph (j) confirms that the Commissioner is able to publish a report on any matter that he or she has considered or investigated under the Commissioner's primary function. It will be for the Commissioner to determine whether to publish a report.

437. Section 2(4) requires the Commissioner - when exercising the primary function - to have particular regard to promoting and protecting the rights of: the categories of children defined in new section 8A (certain vulnerable children); and other children whom the Commissioner determines are at particular risk of their rights being infringed. The definition of children in section 8A (inserted into the 2004 Act by section 114) covers children and young people who previously fell within the remit of the Children's Rights Director, whose general functions are incorporated into those of the Commissioner by this Act. This includes children receiving social care services or who live away from home for significant periods of time, such as children in residential special schools, residential FE colleges and boarding schools.

438. In addition, there are other groups of children who may be at particular risk of having their rights infringed – for example children in custody. Section 2(4) therefore also requires the Commissioner to give particular attention to groups of children who are at particular risk of their rights being infringed. It is for the Commissioner to determine which other groups of children fall within this subsection, and how to act in order to promote and protect their rights.

439. Section 2(5) provides that the Commissioner continues to be prohibited from conducting investigations into the case of an individual child. The intention is that the Commissioner will concentrate on strategic issues that affect a number of children, rather than provide a general ombudsman service for individual children. There may be circumstances however where the Commissioner could properly respond to queries from or about individual children that are relevant to the exercise of the primary function. The Commissioner will be able to provide advice and assistance (as set out in section 2D) to children defined in section 8A.

2A United Nations Convention on the Rights of the Child (UNCRC)

440. Section 2A(1) (inserted into the 2004 Act by section 107) provides that the Commissioner must have particular regard to the UNCRC and any Optional Protocols which are in force in relation to the United Kingdom (subject to any reservations, objections or interpretative declarations by the United Kingdom), when considering what constitutes children's rights and interests. As Article 41 of the UNCRC makes clear, where other rights exist in domestic law or international law applicable to that State, which afford children greater protection than the UNCRC, these should apply.

Section 2B: Involving children in the discharge of the primary function

441. Section 2B (inserted into the 2004 Act by section 107) requires the Commissioner to take reasonable steps to involve children in his or her work, and to provide children with information about the Commissioner's role and how they can raise issues with him or her. Provision is made for children to be consulted on the activities that the Commissioner intends to undertake in the discharge of the primary function. Section 2B(3) requires the Commissioner (when involving children in the discharge of the primary function) to have particular regard to children within new section 8A, and children who do not have other adequate means to make their views known. It will be for the Commissioner to determine which children fall into the latter category.

442. It is for the Commissioner to decide how best to make children aware of his or her role and activities, and to put in place arrangements that allow children to

contact the Commissioner and comment on his or her proposed work programme. The Commissioner may also wish to use other organisations which have an interest in children's rights as a conduit for seeking the views of children, to avoid duplication and to make best use of available resources.

Section 2C: Primary function: reports

443. New section 2C (inserted into the 2004 Act by section 107) relates to reports that the Commissioner publishes following any investigations that he or she has undertaken in carrying out the primary function. Subsection (2) requires the Commissioner to publish a report in a child-friendly format where the Commissioner considers it appropriate to do so. Under subsection (3), it is open to the Commissioner to require persons exercising functions of a public nature to set out in writing, within a time period specified by the Commissioner, what action they are taking or proposing to take in response to recommendations. A person is not obliged to accept recommendations that the Commissioner makes, but if they do not intend to implement a recommendation, they should set out in writing the reasons for not doing so.

Section 108: Provision by Commissioner of advice and assistance to certain children

444. New section 2D (inserted into the 2004 Act by section 80) provides for a new power that enables the Commissioner to provide advice and assistance to children and young people defined in new section 8A. This enables the role previously carried out by the Children's Rights Director to be carried forward under the new arrangements. Section 116 provides for the abolition of the office of Children's Rights Director, alongside relevant transfers to the Commissioner's office.

445. In practice, it is not envisaged that this will involve providing a full casework function. The advice and assistance role will normally entail signposting the individual to an existing complaints process, or making representations on their behalf to the relevant organisation, with a view to resolving the matter informally.

Section 109: Commissioner's power to enter premises

446. This section inserts a new section 2E into the 2004 Act. This broadly replicates the Commissioner's previous power to enter premises where children are accommodated or cared for, in order to interview children, and applies to the exercise of the primary function and new section 2D. This provision does not extend to private dwellings, but applies in respect of any part of a premises which is not a private dwelling. New section 2E(2)(b) and 2E(4) provide that the Commissioner or his or her representative can observe the facilities and standards of care provided and interview persons working at the establishment. These provisions have no impact on the Commissioner's capacity to interview children in situations other than where the power to enter premises is being used.

Section 110: Provision of information to Commissioner

447. This section inserts a new section 2F into the 2004 Act, which broadly replicates the previous provision. It places a duty upon persons exercising functions of a public nature to provide the Commissioner with information that the Commissioner requests as long as: the request is reasonable; and it is information that the body is able to disclose lawfully to the Commissioner. The effect of section 2F is, for example, that where a person exercising functions of a public nature has discretion to disclose confidential information under other legislation, it must do so, so long as the request is reasonable. However, it does not create a legal gateway that overrides other legislation, for example, where that legislation restricts disclosure of confidential information to certain specified persons or for certain purposes.

Section 111: Advisory board

448. New section 7A (inserted into the 2004 Act by section 111) imposes a new requirement on the Children's Commissioner to appoint an advisory board, the purpose of which is to provide advice and assistance to the Commissioner. It is for the Children's Commissioner to decide who to appoint to the board, but subsection (2) requires the board's membership, when taken together, to represent a broad range of interests that are relevant to the functions of the Children's Commissioner. The role of the board is advisory only and ultimately it will be the responsibility of the Children's Commissioner (rather than the advisory board) to determine how to exercise his or her functions. The aim of the advisory board is to make the Commissioner's business planning processes more transparent and to ensure that his or her activities add value, rather than duplicate, the work of other organisations with an interest in children's rights. It is for the Children's Commissioner to determine whether to appoint a separate chairperson from among the members of the advisory board, or to chair the advisory board him or herself. Subsection (3) requires the Commissioner to publish details of the process through which appointments to the advisory board will be made and the criteria used to select members. The intention is to ensure that the process by which individuals are selected is open and transparent.

Section 112: Business plans

449. New section 7B (inserted into the 2004 Act by section 112) imposes requirements on the Children's Commissioner to consult on, and then publish, a business plan. Subsection (1) sets out what should be included in the business plan. Subsections (2) and (3) set out the time period that the business plan should cover and when it should be published. Subsection (4) requires the Commissioner to consult children and bodies which represent a range of relevant interests and other persons who the Commissioner considers appropriate on the content of the business plan before it is published. Subsection (5) provides that when consulting children, the Commissioner should, in particular, take steps to consult children falling within section 8A and other children who do not have adequate means to make their views known.

Section 113: Annual reports

450. This section amends section 8 of the 2004 Act, which is concerned with the Commissioner's annual report. The annual report provides a key mechanism through which Parliament has the opportunity to scrutinise the Commissioner's activities and impact. The annual report provides an overview of the Commissioner's activities rather than being a vehicle through which the Commissioner makes recommendations for change in specific areas; which will be contained in the separate reports that the Commissioner chooses to publish following his or her investigations or inquiries.

451. Accordingly, section 8 requires the Commissioner to report annually on the main activities that he or she has undertaken and what impact these activities have had on the promotion and protection of children's rights. New subsection (2)(b) and (c) require the Commissioner to include in the annual report information on: the actions that he or she has taken to support children falling within section 8A; and an account of how the Commissioner has consulted or otherwise involved children in the discharge of his or her functions.

452. *Subsection (2)(a)* of the section amends section 8(1) of the 2004 Act to provide that the annual report must address how the Commissioner has discharged all his functions. New subsection (2)(d) has been included to ensure that actions the Commissioner takes as a result of consulting or otherwise involving children are also summarised in the annual report. *Subsections (4)* and *(5)* provide for the Commissioner to lay the annual report before both Houses of Parliament, rather than through the Secretary of State, as was previously the case. The Commissioner is responsible for publishing, publicising

and disseminating the report, as appropriate. *Subsection (6)* requires the Commissioner to ensure that a child-friendly version of the annual report is available.

Section 114: Children living away from home or receiving social care

453. This section inserts a new section 8A which defines, for the purposes of the Commissioner's functions, specific groups of children and young people whom the Commissioner:

- Should have particular regard to, when discharging the Commissioner's primary function (as set out in section 2(4));
- Should have particular regard to, when taking steps to involve children in the discharge of the Commissioner's primary function (as set out in section 2B);
- Can provide advice and assistance to (as set out in section 2D);
- Should have particular regard to, when consulting on the Commissioner's business plan (as set out in section 7B(5)).

454. The annual report must also set out how the Commissioner has had particular regard to this group, in exercising his or her functions.

455. The children defined by this section includes all those children and young people who previously fell under the remit of the Children's Rights Director.

Section 115 and Schedule 5: Minor and consequential amendments

456. Schedule 5 makes minor and consequential amendments to Part 1 of the Children Act 2004, and a consequential amendment to the Criminal Justice and Courts Services Act 2000.

Inquiries

457. *Paragraph 1(2)* of Schedule 5 removes the requirement on the Commissioner to consult the Secretary of State before holding an inquiry under section 3 of the 2004 Act; and *paragraph 2(1)* removes the Secretary of State's power to direct the Commissioner to conduct an inquiry. *Paragraph 2(2)* makes consequential amendments to provisions in the 2004 Act that remove the power of the Secretary of State to direct the Commissioner to undertake an inquiry into the case of an individual child in Wales, Scotland or Northern Ireland. The purpose of these changes is to address concerns raised by John Dunford and others which called into question the Commissioner's independence from Government which had potentially damaged the Commissioner's credibility. It will be for the Commissioner to determine how to respond to a request from the Secretary of State to undertake a particular activity.

Functions of Commissioner in respect of Wales, Scotland and Northern Ireland

458. *Paragraphs 3, 4*and*5* amend sections 5, 6 and 7 of the 2004 Act to apply (with certain modifications) the changes to the Commissioner's functions to his or her functions in respect of non-devolved matters in Northern Ireland, Scotland and Wales.

Young persons

459. *Paragraph 6(1)* substitutes a new section 9 in the 2004 Act. Its purpose is to enable the Commissioner to exercise his or her functions in relation to young persons in England who are aged 18 or over for whom an EHC plan is maintained by a local authority (as to which, see Part 3 of the Act); who are aged 18 or over and under 25 and to whom services have been provided by a local authority under any of sections 23C to 24D (which relates to certain children and young people defined in section 8A) of the Children Act 1989.

460. New section 9(3) makes provision in respect of the Commissioner's functions in Wales, Scotland and Northern Ireland. In this case, a child includes a young person who is aged 18 or over and under 25 who has a learning disability (as defined); or who has been looked after by a local authority in Wales, Scotland or Northern Ireland at any time after the age of 16.

461. *Paragraph 6(2)* is intended to preserve the effect of section 9 as it applied before substitution under this Act.

Appointment and tenure of the Children's Commissioner

462. *Paragraph 7* of Schedule 5 amends paragraph 3(2) of Schedule 1 to the 2004 Act, strengthening the requirement on the Secretary of State to involve children in the Commissioner's appointment, by requiring him or her to "take reasonable steps" to involve them.

463. Provision is also made to address a concern raised in John Dunford's report, "Review of the Office of the Children's Commissioner (England)", namely that the ability for a Commissioner to be appointed for a second term might compromise his or her independence. The Children's Commissioner will be now appointed for a single, six-year term. There is no longer an option to renew the Commissioner's appointment at the end of his or her term of office.

Interim Appointments

464. *Paragraph 8* inserts a new paragraph 3A into Schedule 1 to the 2004 Act, which makes provision for appointing an interim Children's Commissioner and sets out the process that should be followed. This provision is introduced as a consequence of removing the requirement on the Commissioner to appoint a Deputy Children's Commissioner and will apply where the current Children's Commissioner resigns, is dismissed (in line with the provisions set out in paragraph 3(7) of Schedule 1 to the 2004 Act), or is otherwise unable to continue in post.

465. Where such a situation arises, a recruitment exercise to appoint a new substantive Children's Commissioner should begin at the earliest opportunity. However, it is possible that recruiting a new substantive Children's Commissioner could take some time and *paragraph 8* therefore provides for the Secretary of State to appoint an interim Children's Commissioner to provide continuity and stability in the intervening period. *Sub-paragraph (2)* provides that the terms and conditions of any interim appointment will be determined by the Secretary of State.

466. Paragraph 3(3) provides that the interim appointment should cease either:

- At the point that a new substantive Commissioner is appointed; or,
- If sooner, 6 months after the date that the interim appointment is made.

467. If, for any reason, the recruitment of a new substantive Commissioner cannot be completed within 6 months, *sub-paragraph (4)* enables the Secretary of State to renew the interim appointment for up to a further 6 months. *Sub-paragraph (4)* also provides that a person who has been appointed as the interim Children's Commissioner can subsequently be appointed as the new substantive Commissioner (following the process required under *paragraph 3* of Schedule 1).

468. Paragraph 3(5) and (6) make provision in relation to resignation and removal from office of the interim Children's Commissioner which is equivalent to the provision for the Children's Commissioner.

Deputy Children's Commissioner

469. *Paragraph 9* amends paragraph 5 of Schedule 1 to the 2004 Act, so as to remove the requirement on the Commissioner to appoint a deputy. It will be for the Commissioner to determine his or her office's staffing structure. *Paragraph 9(2)* makes consequential amendments.

Section 116: Repeal of requirement to appoint a Children's Rights Director

470. *Subsection (1)* repeals the provision in the Education and Inspections Act 2006 which required the Chief Inspector to appoint a Children's Rights Director.

471. *Subsection (2)* amends provisions in that Act to take account of this change and, in particular, to place requirements on the Chief Inspector and the Office for Standards in Education, Children's Services and Skills (Ofsted) to have regard to any matters raised by the Children's Commissioner. In general, the purpose of these provisions is to ensure that the views and interests of children within the Children's Rights Director's remit continue to inform the work of the Chief Inspector and the Office for Standards in Education, Children's Services and Skills but they will also extend more generally to cover any matters raised by the Children's Commissioner.

472. *Subsection (3)* introduces Schedule 6, which provides for the Secretary of State to make a scheme enabling certain staff and property to be transferred from Ofsted to the staff of the Children's Commissioner.

Schedule 6: Repeal of requirement to appoint a Children's Rights Director: Transfer schemes

473. *Paragraph 1* contains a power for the Secretary of State to make a scheme in relation to designated members of staff who are members of staff of Ofsted to become members of staff of the Children's Commissioner. The Schedule provides that the scheme may contain provisions as to continuity of employment.

474. *Paragraph 2* contains a power for the Secretary of State to make a property transfer scheme, transferring to the Children's Commissioner any property, rights and liabilities of Ofsted.

475. *Paragraph 3* provides that for the purposes of the transfer schemes, references to "the Office" (i.e. Ofsted) include, so far as relevant, the Chief Inspector.

Part 7 - Statutory Rights to Leave and Pay

Shared parental leave

Section 117: Shared parental leave

476. This section inserts a new Chapter 1B into Part 8 of the Employment Rights Act 1996 (ERA). This creates a new entitlement for employees to be absent from work on shared parental leave for the purposes of caring for a child.

Section 75E: Entitlement to shared parental leave: birth

477. Section 75E deals with entitlement to shared parental leave in relation to birth.

478. Subsections (1) and (4) confer powers on the Secretary of State to make regulations entitling employees to be absent from work for the purpose of caring for a child if they satisfy certain specified conditions.

479. Subsections (1) to (3) are about the conditions for eligibility of the mother of the child. The conditions that may be specified include conditions as to duration of employment, her relationship with the child and as to caring with another person ("P") for the child.

Subsection (1)(f) includes a condition relating to the giving of a notice of intention to take shared parental leave; and subsection (3) specifies what this notice may be about: it may be about the amount of leave available to the mother; the amount of leave the mother intends to take; and whether and to what extent P will take leave or statutory shared parental pay. Subsection (1)(g) specifies a condition relating to the consent of P to the amount of leave that the mother intends to take.

480. Subsection (2) provides that the conditions of entitlement of the mother can include P meeting conditions in respect of P's employment or self-employment, P's earnings, P's relationship to the mother or the child and P's intention to care, with the mother, for the child. The effect of this provision is that one of the conditions of entitlement to shared parental leave for the mother can relate to the mother's sharing the care of the child with P and P satisfying conditions as to economic activity and relationship with the child or the mother.

481. Subsection (4) specifies conditions that may be included in regulations to give entitlement to shared parental leave for another employee (the father or the mother's partner). These include certain conditions as to duration of employment, the employee's relationship with the child or with the child's mother and as to the employee caring, with the child's mother, for the child. Subsection (4)(d) includes a condition relating to the giving of a notice of intention to take shared parental leave. Subsection (4)(e) specifies a condition relating to the child's mother's consent to the amount of shared parental leave the employee intends to take.

482. Subsection (5) provides that the conditions of entitlement for the employee can include the mother meeting conditions as to her employment or self-employment, her earnings, her caring with the employee for the child and her entitlement (or otherwise) to statutory maternity pay or maternity allowance and the exercise of these entitlements. The effect of this provision is that one of the conditions of entitlement to shared parental leave for an employee (the father or the mother's partner) can relate to the employee sharing care of the child with the mother and to the mother satisfying conditions as to economic activity.

483. Subsection (6) specifies what the notice the employee is required to give under subsection (4) is about. It may be about the amount of leave available to the employee, the amount of leave the employee intends to take, and whether and to what extent the mother will take leave or shared parental pay.

Section 75F: Entitlement to leave under section 75E: further provision

484. Section 75F is about the making of regulations to calculate the amount of leave available to the employee, to limit the amount of shared parental leave, to limit when it may be taken, to require the leave to be taken as a single period and to provide for the varying of the amount of shared parental leave that an employee may take and the times at which an employee takes this leave.

485. This section provides that regulations under section 75E will include provisions for determining the amount of shared parental leave and when this leave may be taken. Subsection (7) specifies that provision under subsection (1)(b) is to secure that shared parental leave must be taken before the end of such a period as may be prescribed. Subsection (8) further specifies that provision under subsection (1)(b) is to provide for the taking of shared parental leave in a single period or in non-consecutive periods.

486. This section specifies the maximum amount of leave to which an employee is entitled. The maximum amount in the case of a mother who is entitled to maternity leave is an amount of time specified by regulations (expected to be the total length of maternity leave (52 weeks)) less the amount of maternity leave taken by the mother (where she returns to work without taking specified action to reduce her maternity leave period) or the amount by which the maternity leave period has been reduced. The maximum amount of time in the case of a mother who is entitled to statutory maternity pay or

maternity allowance only is an amount of time specified by regulations (expected to be 52 weeks) less the number of weeks of statutory maternity pay or maternity allowance payable to the child's mother, or the number of weeks by which the maternity allowance period or maternity pay period has been reduced.

487. This section specifies that the amount of shared parental leave to which the employee is entitled in respect of a child takes into account the amount of such leave taken by another person in respect of that child or the number of weeks of statutory shared parental pay received by another person in respect of that child (in the case where the other person is entitled to statutory shared parental pay in respect of the child but not to shared parental leave).

488. This section specifies that for the purposes of calculation of the amount of shared parental leave under this section, part of a week is to be treated as a full week.

489. This section provides that the regulations under section 75E may enable an employer, in a case where an employee has proposed to take non-consecutive periods of shared parental leave, to require the employee to take that amount of leave as a single period of leave. This single period of leave may start with a day proposed by the employee or, if no day is proposed, with the first day of the first period of leave proposed by the employee. This provision is to provide a default position for when the shared parental leave can be taken if agreement cannot be reached between employer and employee.

490. This section provides that regulations made under section 75E may enable an employee, subject to prescribed restrictions, to vary the period or periods of shared parental leave to be taken without varying the amount of leave, and to vary the amount of leave which the employee has notified an intention to exercise. This section provides that variations to the period or periods during which the leave is taken may require this variation to be subject to obtaining the employer's consent in circumstances specified by regulations. This section specifies that in relation to variations to the amount of leave which the employee has notified an intention to exercise, the employee may be required to do this by notice and the consent of the child's mother or P may be required. This section specifies that notifications of variation of the amount of leave which an employee intends to exercise may be required to include notice about the amount of shared parental leave the employee has taken in respect of the child, how much leave the employee intends to take and the amount of shared parental leave or statutory shared parental pay that the other person who may be entitled to such leave or pay in respect of the child, has taken or intends to take.

491. This section provides that regulations made under section 75E may specify: the things which are and are not to be taken as done for the purpose of caring for the child; the minimum amount of shared parental leave that may be taken and provision about how this leave may be taken; the circumstances in which an employee may work for an employer during a period of shared parental leave without bringing the period of leave, or the employee's entitlement to it, to an end; and the circumstances in which the employee may be absent on shared parental leave otherwise than for the purpose of caring for a child without bringing their entitlement to an end. The latter provision might be relevant to situations where an employee has an entitlement to shared parental leave but whose child subsequently dies. They may also make provision to exclude the right to be absent on shared parental leave in respect of a child where more than one child is born as a result of the same pregnancy.

492. This section enables the Secretary of State to provide by regulations that certain subsections do not have effect, or have effect with prescribed modifications, in a case where the mother of a child dies before another person has become entitled to shared parental leave in respect of that child. This might be relevant to situations where a mother dies before entitlement to shared parental leave has arisen for herself or her partner.

Section 75G: Entitlement to shared parental leave: adoption

493. Section 75G deals with entitlement to shared parental leave in relation to adoption.

494. Subsections (1) and (4) confer powers on the Secretary of State to make regulations entitling employees who are adopters or prospective adopters to be absent from work for the purpose of caring for a child if they satisfy certain conditions.

495. Subsections (1) to (3) are about the conditions of eligibility of the person with whom a child is to be, or is expected to be, placed for adoption (the "primary adopter"). These include certain conditions as to the primary adopter's duration of employment, relationship with the child and as to caring with another person ("P") for the child. Subsection (1)(g) specifies a condition relating to the consent of P to the amount of leave the primary adopter intends to take. Subsection (1)(f) includes a condition relating to the giving of a notice of intention to take shared parental leave under this subsection; and subsection (3) specifies what this notice may be about, such as the maximum amount of leave available to the primary adopter, the amount of leave the primary adopter intends to take and the extent to which P intends to exercise entitlement to the leave or to statutory shared parental pay.

496. Subsection (2) provides that the conditions of entitlement of the primary adopter can include P meeting certain conditions in respect of employment or self-employment, earnings, relationship to the primary adopter or the child and having caring responsibility for the child. The effect of this provision is that one of the conditions of entitlement to shared parental leave for the primary adopter can relate to the primary adopter sharing the care of the child with P and P satisfying conditions as to economic activity and relation with the child or the primary adopter.

497. Subsections (4) to (6) specify conditions that may be included in regulations to give entitlement to shared parental leave to another employee (other than the primary adopter). These include certain conditions as to duration of employment, the employee's relationship with the child and with the primary adopter and as to the employee caring with the primary adopter for the child. Subsection (4)(d) includes a condition relating to giving notice of intention to take shared parental leave. Subsection (4)(e) specifies a condition relating to the consent of the primary adopter to the amount of leave that the other employee intends to take.

498. Subsection (5) provides that the conditions for entitlement for the employee can include the primary adopter meeting conditions as to employment or self-employment and earnings; the primary adopter caring with the employee for the child; the primary adopter's entitlement (or otherwise) to adoption leave or statutory adoption pay, and the extent of the primary adopter's exercise of such entitlement.

499. Subsection (6) specifies what the notice the employee is required to give under subsection (4) is about. It may be about the maximum possible extent of their entitlement to leave, the amount of leave the employee intends to take, and whether and to what extent the primary adopter will exercise an entitlement to shared parental leave or statutory shared parental pay.

Section 75H: Entitlement to leave under section 75G: further provision

500. Section 75H is about the making of regulations to calculate the amount of shared parental leave available to the employee, to limit the amount of shared parental leave, to limit when it may be taken, to require the leave to be taken as a single period and to provide for the varying of the amount of shared parental leave that an employee may take and the times at which an employee takes this leave.

501. This section provides that regulations under section 75G will include provisions for determining the amount of shared parental leave to which an employee is entitled in respect of a child, and when this leave may be taken. This section specifies that provision under subsection (1)(b) is to allow shared parental leave to be taken in non-

consecutive periods. The effect of this is to allow the leave to be taken more flexibly than in a single consecutive block.

502. This section specifies the maximum amount of leave to which an employee is entitled. The maximum amount in the case of a primary adopter who is entitled to adoption leave is an amount of time specified in regulations (expected to be the total length of adoption leave (52 weeks)) less the amount of adoption leave taken by the primary adopter (where the primary adopter returns to work without taking specified action to reduce the adoption leave period) or the amount by which the adoption leave period has been reduced. The maximum amount of time in the case of a primary adopter who is entitled to statutory adoption pay only is an amount of time specified by regulations (expected to be 52 weeks) less the number of weeks of statutory adoption pay payable to the primary adopter, or the number of weeks by which the adoption pay period has been reduced. Subsection (3) specifies that the amount of shared parental leave to which the employee is entitled in respect of a child takes into account the amount of such leave taken by another person in respect of that child, or the number of weeks of statutory shared parental pay received by the other person in respect of the child (in a case where the other person is entitled to statutory shared parental pay in respect of the child but not shared parental leave.)

503. This section specifies that provision under subsection (1)(b) is to secure that shared parental leave must be taken before the end of a prescribed period.

504. This section specifies that for the purposes of calculating the amount of adoption leave or shared parental leave taken, part of a week is to be treated as a full week.

505. This section provides that the regulations under section 75G may enable an employer, in a case where an employee has proposed to take non-consecutive periods of shared parental leave, to require the employee to take that amount of leave as a single period of leave. This single period of leave will start with a day proposed by the employee or, if no day is proposed, with the first day of the first period of leave proposed by the employee. The effect of this provision is to provide a default position for when shared parental leave can be taken if agreement cannot be reached between employer and employee.

506. This section provides that regulations made under section 75G may enable an employee, subject to prescribed restrictions, to vary the period(s) of shared parental leave to be taken without varying the amount of leave and to vary the amount of leave which the employee has notified an intention to exercise. This section provides that variations to the period or periods during which the leave is taken may require this variation to be subject to obtaining the employer's consent in circumstances specified by regulations. This section specifies that in relation to variations to the amount of leave which the employee has notified an intention to exercise, the employee may be required to include certain information in the notice to their employer and the consent of the primary adopter or P (as appropriate) may be required. This section specifies that notifications of variation of the amount of leave which an employee intends to exercise may be required to include notice about the amount of shared parental leave the employee has taken in respect of the child, how much leave the employee intends to take and the amount of shared parental leave or statutory shared parental pay that the other person who may be entitled to such leave or pay in respect of the child, has taken or intends to take.

507. This section provides that regulations made under section 75G may specify the things which are and are not to be taken as done for the purpose of caring for the child; the minimum amount of shared parental leave that may be taken and provision about how this leave may be taken; the circumstances in which an employee may work for an employer during a period of shared parental leave without bringing the period of leave, or the employee's entitlement to it, to an end and the circumstances in which the employee may be absent on shared parental leave otherwise than for the purpose of caring for a child without bringing their entitlement to an end. The latter may be relevant to situations where an employee has an entitlement to shared parental leave but whose child subsequently dies. They may also make provision to ensure that an

employee cannot take more than one period of shared parental leave in circumstances where more than one child is placed for adoption as part of the same arrangement.

508. This section specifies that in this section "week" means any period of seven days.

509. This section enables regulations to stipulate that certain subsections do not have effect, or have effect with prescribed modifications, in a case where the person who is taking adoption leave or is entitled to be paid statutory adoption pay dies before another person has become entitled to shared parental leave in respect of the relevant child. This is to enable the other person to be able to become entitled to shared parental leave after the death of the primary adopter.

510. This section allows the Secretary of State to provide for sections 75G and 75H to have effect, with appropriate modifications, in relation to cases where a child has been adopted under the laws of a jurisdiction outside the United Kingdom.

511. This section enables the Secretary of State to provide by means of regulations for sections 75G and 75H to have effect (with modifications) in relation to cases involving an employee who has applied, or intends to apply, with another person, under section 54 of the Human Fertilisation and Embryology Act 2008 for a parental order in respect of a child ("intended parent"). This will allow some parents in surrogacy arrangements to be entitled to shared parental leave in the same way as certain adoptive parents.

Section 75I: Rights during and after shared parental leave

512. Section 75I deals with the rights of employees during and after shared parental leave.

513. Subsection (1) provides for regulations under section 75E or 75G to specify the rights and responsibilities of employees whilst on, and after shared parental leave. Subsection (1)(a) states that employees who are absent on shared parental leave will be entitled as far as prescribed, to the benefit of the same terms and conditions of employment which would have applied if the employee had not been absent.

514. Subsection (1)(b) further stipulates that whilst on shared parental leave the employee will continue to be bound, as far as prescribed, by the obligations that would arise from those terms and conditions, to the extent they are compatible with the taking of shared parental leave.

515. Subsection (1)(c) provides for an employee who has been absent on shared parental leave to have the right to return to a kind of job as specified in regulations. Subsection (5) provides for regulations to make provision about seniority, pension and other similar rights, and terms and conditions of employment on return.

516. Subsection (3) stipulates that, where appropriate, the type of absence that gives rise to the right to return referenced in subsection (1)(c) may be a continuous period of absence attributable to a combination of shared parental leave, maternity leave, paternity leave, adoption leave and parental leave.

517. Subsection (2)(b) specifies that "terms and conditions of employment" as referenced in subsection (1)(a) does not include remuneration. Subsection (4) provides that regulations may specify matters which are or are not to be treated as remuneration for the purpose of entitlement to shared parental leave (for birth and adoption).

Section 75J: Redundancy and dismissal

518. Section 75J provides that regulations under section 75E or 75G may make provisions about redundancy or dismissal during a period of shared parental leave.

519. Subsection (2) states that such provisions may include a requirement for an employer to offer alternative employment, and provision for the consequences of failure to comply with the regulations.

Section 75K: Chapter 1B: supplemental

520. Section 75K allows regulations to be made about notices, evidence, procedures to be followed and other supplementary matters.

521. Subsection (1)(a) enables regulations to provide for notices to be given, evidence to be produced and other procedures to be followed by employers, employees and relevant persons. Subsection (2) defines "relevant person". Subsection (1)(b) enables regulations to require such persons to keep records. Subsection (1)(c) enables regulations to provide for the consequences of failure to give notices, produce evidence, keep records or comply with other procedural requirements. Subsection (1)(d) enables regulations to make provision for the consequences of failure to act in accordance with such a notice. Subsection (1)(e) enables special provision for cases to be made where an employee has a right which corresponds to a right to shared parental leave and which arises under the employee's contract of employment or otherwise. Subsection (1)(f) and (g) allows for regulations to make provision to modify provision in the ERA relating to the calculation of a week's pay and to modify, apply or exclude enactments in relation to a person entitled to shared parental leave.

522. Subsections (3) to (5) ensure that the conditions of economic activity which may be specified under sections 75E(2) or (5) and 75G(2) or (5) in relation to the person with whom care of the child is shared can include conditions relating to that person being an employed earner or a self-employed earner. They also ensure that the power to make provision about procedures to be followed by an employer of that other person under section 75K includes, as far as concerns an employed earner, the secondary contributor (in relation to secondary Class I National Insurance contributions).

523. Subsection (6) allows for regulations under any of sections 75E to 75H to make different provision for different cases or circumstances.

524. Subsection (7) provides that the Secretary of State can prescribe that eligible intended parents in surrogacy arrangements who wish to take shared parental leave must make a statutory declaration as to their eligibility and intention to apply for a parental order.

Section 118: Exclusion or curtailment of other statutory rights to leave

525. This section amends the ERA to allow regulations to be made which will enable a birth mother or primary adopter to bring their ordinary maternity or adoption leave to an end early. This will allow the person and/or their partner to access the new system of shared parental leave and pay.

526. This section allows regulations to be made which will set out the circumstances in which the birth mother or adoptive parent can change their mind about a decision to end their ordinary maternity or adoption leave early. It is intended that the birth mother will be able to revoke a decision made before the birth until a certain point (which will be set out in the regulations) after the birth.

527. This section provides that these regulations may only allow a birth mother or adoptive parent to bring their ordinary maternity or adoption leave to an end if they and the person with whom they share care of the child take certain steps in relation to the taking of shared parental leave or pay which will include giving notice to their employers where relevant.

528. This section also allows regulations to be made which will enable a birth mother or primary adopter to bring their additional maternity or adoption leave to an end early. It mirrors the provisions for ordinary maternity leave which are described above.

529. Finally, this section requires regulations to be made which will provide that the taking of shared parental leave prevents an employee from exercising the right to take any remaining paternity leave. This applies in both birth and adoption cases.

Statutory shared parental pay

Section 119: Statutory shared parental pay

530. This section inserts a new Part 12ZC into the Social Security Contributions and Benefits Act 1992 (SSCBA), enabling regulations to be made to create new entitlements to shared parental pay for qualifying birth parents, adopters and intended parents in surrogacy arrangements.

Section 171ZU: Entitlement: birth

531. This section deals with entitlement to statutory shared parental pay in relation to birth.

532. Subsection (1) confers power on the Secretary of State to make regulations to provide that where the conditions in subsection (2) are satisfied, the mother of a child (the "claimant mother") is entitled to payments to be known as "statutory shared parental pay".

533. The condition in subsection (2)(a) is that the claimant mother and another person ("P") satisfy certain prescribed conditions as to caring or intending to care for the child.

534. The condition in subsection (2)(b) is that P must meet certain prescribed conditions as to employment or self-employment, earnings and relationship with the claimant mother or child. The conditions in subsection (2)(c), (d) and (e) require the claimant mother to have met prescribed conditions regarding a continuous length of employment, earnings and entitlement to be in employment. The condition in subsection (2)(f) is that, if regulations so provide, the claimant mother continues in employed earner's employment until such a time as specified.

535. The condition in subsection (2)(g) is that the claimant mother became entitled to receive statutory maternity pay in respect of the child. The condition in subsection (2)(h) relates to the reduction of the maternity pay period applying to the claimant mother.

536. The condition in subsection (2)(i) and (j) is that the claimant mother has given notice of the total number of weeks which she would be entitled to claim statutory shared parental pay, the number of weeks she intends to claim the pay and the number of weeks P intends to claim the pay and the periods during which the claimant mother intends to claim the pay.

537. The condition in subsection (2)(k) is that the notices under subsection (2)(i) and (j) are given by such a time as may be prescribed and satisfy certain prescribed conditions as to form and content

538. The condition in subsection (2)(l) is that P consents to the amount of statutory shared parental pay the claimant mother intends to claim.

539. The condition in subsection (2)(m) is that it must be the claimant mother's intention to care for the child during each week in which statutory shared parental pay is paid to her.

540. The conditions in subsection (2)(n) and (o) state the claimant mother must be absent from work for each week that statutory shared parental pay is paid to her. Where she is an employee, she must be absent from work on shared parental leave.

541. Subsection (3) confers power on the Secretary of State to make regulations to provide that where the conditions in subsection (4) are satisfied, a person ("the claimant") is entitled to payments to be known as "statutory shared parental pay".

542. The condition in subsection (4)(a) is that the claimant and another person who is the mother of a child satisfy certain prescribed conditions as to caring or intending to care for the child. The condition in subsection (4)(b) is that the claimant must satisfy certain prescribed conditions as to the relationship with the child or the child's mother.

543. The condition in subsection (4)(c) is that the child's mother meets prescribed conditions as to employment or self-employment and earnings. The conditions in subsection (4)(d), (e) and (f) are that the claimant has met prescribed conditions relating to a continuous length of employment, earnings and entitlement to be in that employment. The condition in subsection (4)(g) is that the claimant, if so prescribed, must continue in employed earner's employment until such a time as specified in regulations.

544. The condition in subsection (4)(h) is that the mother of the child must have been entitled as a result of the birth of the child to receive either maternity allowance or statutory maternity pay. The condition in subsection (4)(i) relates to the reduction of the maternity pay period or the maternity allowance period applying to the mother.

545. The condition in subsection (4)(j) and (k) is that the claimant has given notice of the total number of weeks which the claimant would be entitled to claim statutory shared parental pay, the number of weeks the claimant intends to claim the pay and the number of weeks the child's mother intends to claim the pay and the periods during which the claimant intends to claim the pay.

546. The condition in subsection (4)(l) is that the notices are submitted by such a time as may be prescribed and satisfy prescribed conditions as to form and content. The condition in subsection (4)(m) is that the mother of the child must consent to the amount of statutory shared parental pay that the claimant intends to claim.

547. The condition in subsection (4)(n) is that it is the claimant's intention to care for the child during each week in which statutory shared parental pay is paid to the claimant.

548. The condition in subsection (4)(o) and (p) is that the claimant must be absent from work for each week that statutory shared parental pay is paid to the claimant. If the claimant is an employee, the claimant must be absent from work on shared parental leave.

549. Subsection (5) provides for the Secretary of State to make regulations to determine the extent of a person's entitlement to statutory shared parental pay in respect of a child, and the times at which this is to be paid.

550. Subsections (6) and (7) provide the extent of a person's entitlement to statutory shared parental pay cannot exceed the length of the maternity pay period (currently 39 weeks) less the number of weeks that maternity allowance or maternity pay is payable to the mother up to her return to work or the number of weeks by which the maternity pay period or maternity allowance period has been reduced (where the mother reduces these periods before returning to work). Subsection (7) defines the meaning of "relevant week".

551. Subsection (8) specifies that for the purposes of the calculation under subsection (6)(b), part of a week is to be treated as a full week.

552. Subsection (9) specifies that provision under subsection (5)(a) is to ensure that where two people are both entitled to statutory shared parental pay in respect of the same child, the total number of weeks taken by both does not exceed the number of weeks as specified in the calculation described under subsection (6). Subsection (10) specifies that provision under subsection (5)(b) as to when statutory shared parental pay is payable is to ensure that payments of statutory shared parental pay cannot be made to a person after such period as may be prescribed. Subsection (11) further specifies that the provision as to when statutory shared parental pay is payable is to ensure that no payment of statutory shared parental pay may be made to the mother of the child before the end of the mother's maternity pay period.

553. Subsection (12) provides for regulations to enable a person who is entitled to statutory shared parental pay to vary the period or periods during which the person intends to claim such pay without varying the overall amount of statutory shared parental pay the person intends to take, provided certain conditions are satisfied. These conditions are specified in subsection (13). They require the person who intends to claim statutory

shared parental pay to give notice of their intention to vary the period or periods during which they intend to claim the pay to the person who will be liable to pay it. This notice must be given by such time and satisfying certain conditions as to form and content as may be prescribed.

554. Subsection (14) provides for regulations to enable a person who is entitled to statutory shared parental pay to vary the number of weeks that the person intends to claim, providing certain conditions are satisfied. These conditions are specified in subsection (15). They require that the person must give notice of certain specified information to the person who will be liable to pay the statutory shared parental pay. The consent of the other person eligible for statutory shared parental pay in respect of the same child must also be obtained. This notice must be given by such time as may be prescribed and satisfying certain conditions as to form and content.

555. Subsection (16) specifies that a person's entitlement to statutory shared parental pay under this section is not affected by the birth of more than one child as a result of the same pregnancy.

Section 171ZV: Entitlement: adoption

556. This section deals with entitlement to statutory shared parental pay in relation to adoption.

557. Subsections (1) and (3) confer power to make regulations to provide that where the respective conditions in subsections (2) and (4) are satisfied, a person with whom a child is, or is expected to be, placed for adoption ("claimant A") and another person ("claimant B") are to be entitled to payments to be known as "statutory shared parental pay".

558. Subsection (2) of the new section states the conditions claimant A must meet in order to be entitled to statutory shared parental pay. In some cases, the conditions provide for further matters to be dealt with in regulations.

559. The condition in subsection (2)(a) is that claimant A and another person ("X") must satisfy certain prescribed conditions as to caring or intending to care for the child.

560. The condition in subsection (2)(b) specifies that the other person must have met certain prescribed conditions as to employment status, earnings and relationship with claimant A or the child. In practice, X may also be the person who is claimant B for the purposes of subsection (3).

561. The conditions in subsection (2)(c), (d) and (e) require claimant A to have met certain prescribed conditions regarding length of service, earnings and entitlement to be in employment. The condition in subsection (2)(f) is that, if regulations so provide, claimant A must continue in employed earner's employment until such a time as specified in regulations.

562. The condition in subsection (2)(g) is that claimant A became entitled to receive statutory adoption pay in respect of the child. The condition in subsection (2)(h) relates to the reduction of the adoption pay period.

563. The condition in subsection (2)(i) and (j) is that claimant A has given notice of the total number of weeks claimant A would be entitled to claim statutory shared parental pay, the number of weeks claimant A intends to claim the pay, the number of weeks X intends to claim the pay and the periods during which claimant A intends to claim the pay.

564. The condition in subsection (2)(k) is that the notices under subsection (2)(i) or (j) are given by such a time as may be prescribed and satisfy certain prescribed conditions as to form and content.

565. The condition in subsection (2)(l) is that X must consent to the amount of statutory shared parental pay claimant A intends to claim.

566. The condition in subsection (2)(m) specifies that it must be claimant A's intention to care for the child during each week in which statutory shared parental pay is paid to claimant A.

567. The conditions in subsection (2)(n) and (o) are that claimant A must be absent from work for each week that statutory shared parental pay is paid to claimant A. Where claimant A is an employee, that person must be absent from work on shared parental leave.

568. Subsection (4) deals with the conditions that claimant B must meet in order to be entitled to statutory shared parental pay. As with the entitlement criteria for claimant A, in some cases the conditions provide for further matters to be dealt with in regulations.

569. The condition in subsection (4)(a) is that claimant B and another person ("Y") who is a person with whom a child is, or is expecting to be, placed for adoption satisfy certain prescribed conditions as to caring or intending to care for the child. Subsection (4)(b) requires that claimant B satisfy certain conditions as regards relationship with the child or Y. In practice, Y may also be the same person who is claimant A for the purposes of subsection (1).

570. The condition in subsection (4)(c) is that Y must meet certain employment status and earnings criteria, the details of which will be prescribed in regulations. The conditions in subsection (4)(d), (e) and (f) require that claimant B has met certain prescribed conditions relating to a continuous length of employment, earnings and entitlement to be in that employment. The condition in subsection (4)(g) is that claimant B, if so prescribed, must continue in employed earner's employment until such a time as specified in regulations.

571. The condition in subsection (4)(h) is that Y became entitled to receive statutory adoption pay by reference to the child. The condition in subsection (4)(i) relates to the reduction of the adoption pay period applying to Y.

572. The condition in subsection (4)(j) and (k) is that claimant B has given notice of the total number of weeks which claimant B would be entitled to claim statutory shared parental pay, the number of weeks claimant B intends to claim pay and the number of weeks Y intends to claim the pay and the periods during which claimant B intends to claim the pay. The condition in subsection (4)(l) is that these notices be submitted by such a time as may be prescribed and satisfy prescribed conditions as to form and content. The condition in subsection (4)(m) is that Y consent to the amount of statutory shared parental pay that claimant B intends to claim.

573. The condition in subsection (4)(n) is that it must be claimant B's intention to care for the child during each week in which statutory shared parental pay is paid to the claimant.

574. The condition in subsection (4)(o) and (p) is that claimant B must be absent from work for each week that statutory shared parental pay is paid to the claimant. If claimant B is an employee, the claimant must be absent from work on shared parental leave.

575. Subsection (5) provides for the Secretary of State to make regulations to determine the extent of a person's entitlement to statutory shared parental pay in respect of a child, and the times at which this may be paid.

576. Subsections (6) and (7) provide the extent of a person's entitlement to statutory shared parental pay cannot exceed the length of the adoption pay period (currently 39 weeks) less the number of weeks that adoption pay is payable to the claimant's return to work or the number of weeks by which the adoption pay period has been reduced (where the claimant reduces this period before returning to work). Subsection (7) defines the meaning of "relevant week".

577. Subsection (8) further specifies that for the purposes of calculations under subsection (6)(b), part of a week is to be treated as a full week.

578. Subsection (9) specifies that provision under subsection (5)(a) is to ensure that when two people are entitled to statutory shared parental pay in respect of the same child, the total number of weeks taken cannot exceed the number of weeks calculated under subsection (6).

579. Subsection (10) specifies that provision under subsection (5)(b) as to when statutory shared parental pay is payable is to secure that payments of statutory shared parental pay cannot be made to a person after a prescribed period. Subsection (11) further specifies that the provision as to when statutory shared parental pay is payable is to secure that where a person is entitled to receive statutory adoption pay, no payment of statutory shared parental pay may be made to them before the end of their adoption pay period.

580. Subsection (12) provides for regulations to enable a person who is entitled to statutory shared parental pay to vary the period(s) during which the person intends to claim such pay without varying the overall amount of statutory shared parental pay the person intends to take, provided certain conditions are satisfied. These conditions are specified in subsection (13). They require the person who intends to claim statutory shared parental pay to give notice of their intention to vary the period(s) during which they intend to claim the pay to the person who will be liable to pay it. This notice must satisfy certain prescribed conditions as to time, form and content.

581. Subsection (14) provides power to make regulations to enable a person who is entitled to statutory shared parental pay to vary the number of weeks of shared parental pay that he or she intends to claim, providing certain conditions in subsection (15) are satisfied. They require that the person must give notice in prescribed form and by a prescribed time, containing specified information to the person who will be liable to pay the statutory shared parental pay. The consent of the other person eligible for statutory shared parental pay in respect of the same child must also be obtained.

582. Subsection (16) has the effect that if a person adopts more than one child as part of the same arrangement, he or she will not be entitled to take any more shared parental pay than that to which he or she would have been entitled if only one child was adopted.

Section 171ZW: Entitlement: general

583. This section makes further provision about a person's entitlement to statutory shared parental pay (whether in relation to birth or adoption).

584. Subsection (1)(a) provides power for the Secretary of State to provide that the entitlement conditions for statutory shared parental pay do not have effect, or have effect subject to prescribed modifications in such cases as may be prescribed.

585. Subsection (1)(b) provides power for the Secretary of State to impose requirements about evidence of entitlement by way of regulations.

586. Subsection (1)(c) to (f) provides power for the Secretary of State to make provision relating to continuous employment and the calculation of earnings.

587. Subsection (2) defines the person or persons on whom requirements may be imposed by virtue of subsection (1)(b).

Section 171ZX: Liability to make payments

588. This section makes provision about liability to pay statutory shared parental pay (whether in relation to birth or adoption).

589. Subsection (1) of the inserted section provides for employers to be liable for the payment of statutory shared parental pay. (Although under section 7 of the Employment

Act 2002, as amended by Schedule 7, provision is made for the funding of employers' liabilities to pay statutory shared parental pay.)

590. Subsection (2) requires the Secretary of State to make regulations about the liability of a former employer to pay statutory shared parental pay where the employee has been dismissed by the employer to avoid liability to pay statutory shared parental pay.

591. Subsection (3) of the inserted section provides power for the Secretary of State, with the concurrence of the Commissioners for HMRC, to specify in regulations circumstances in which liability for paying statutory shared parental pay is to fall on the Commissioners.

Section 171ZY: Rate and period of pay

592. This section deals with the rate at which statutory shared parental pay is payable and the period for which it is payable (whether in relation to birth or adoption).

Section 171ZZ: Restrictions on contracting out

593. This section deals with restrictions on contracting out.

594. Subsection (1) provides that an agreement is void to the extent that it purports to exclude, limit or otherwise modify any provision of the new Part 12ZC of the SSCBA, or to require a person to contribute (whether directly or indirectly) towards any costs incurred by that person's employer or former employer under that Part.

595. Subsection (2) contains a provision which ensures that certain agreements with an employee authorising deductions from shared parental pay are not void.

Section 171ZZ1: Relationship with contractual remuneration

596. This section deals with the way in which statutory shared parental pay interacts with contractual remuneration.

597. Subsection (1) provides that, subject to subsections (2) and (3), any entitlement to statutory shared parental pay is not to affect any right of any person in relation to contractual remuneration. Subsection (2) specifies that payment of contractual remuneration can be counted as discharging a liability of the employer to pay statutory shared parental pay. Also payment of statutory shared parental pay can be counted as discharging an obligation of the employer to pay contractual remuneration.

598. Subsection (3) makes provision for regulations to provide which payments are to be treated as contractual remuneration for the purposes of subsections (1) and (2).

Section 171ZZ2: Crown employment

599. This section provides that the provisions of the new Part 12ZC of the SSCBA apply in relation to persons employed by or under the Crown in the same way as persons otherwise employed.

Section 171ZZ3: Special classes of person

600. This section gives power to the Secretary of State to make regulations modifying any provision of the Part of the Act dealing with statutory shared parental pay in application to special classes of person. The special classes are those employed on board any ship, vessel, hovercraft or aircraft; outside Great Britain at a prescribed time or in prescribed circumstances; and in prescribed employment in connection with continental shelf operations.

Section 171ZZ4: Part 12ZC: supplementary

601. Subsections (1), (2) and (5) define the meaning of "employer", "modifications", "prescribed", "employee" and "week" in the Part of the Act dealing with statutory shared parental pay.

602. Subsection (3) provides that persons who do not meet the definition of "employee" as stated in subsection (2) may be treated as such for the purposes of the Part of the Act dealing with statutory shared parental pay, and that some who do meet the definition may be treated as if they do not.

603. Subsection (4) provides that two or more employers and that two or more contracts of service in respect of the same employee may be treated as one for the purposes of this Part by way of regulations.

604. Subsection (6) sets out how to calculate a person's normal weekly earnings for the purposes of this new Part 12ZC of the SSCBA. Subsection (7) provides for the meaning of "earnings" and "relevant period" as mentioned in subsection (6) to be defined in regulations. Subsection (8) provides that a person's normal weekly earnings will be calculated in accordance with regulations in such cases as may be prescribed.

605. Subsections (9) to (11) make special provision as to the treatment of contracts of employment within the NHS.

Section 171ZZ5: Power to apply Part 12ZC

606. Subsection (1) enables provision to be made so that the shared parental pay regulations made under the new Part 12ZC of the SSCBA may have effect in relation to cases involving the adoption of a child from outside the jurisdiction of the United Kingdom.

607. Subsection (2) enables provision to be made so that the shared parental pay regulations made under the new Part 12ZC of the SSCBA may have effect in relation to intended parents in surrogacy arrangements who meet certain conditions.

608. Subsection (3) enables regulations made under section 171ZW(1)(b) (about evidence of entitlement and procedures to be followed) to require that intended parents in surrogacy arrangements who wish to take shared parental pay must make statutory declarations as to their eligibility and intention to apply for a parental order.

Section 120: Curtailment of statutory pay periods and exclusion of statutory pay

609. This section amends the SSCBA. It inserts provisions into sections 35, 165 171ZE and 171ZN that allow regulations to be made that will enable the duration of the maternity allowance period, the maternity pay period or the adoption pay period as it applies to a person to be reduced subject to prescribed conditions and restrictions. This will allow access to the new system of shared parental leave and pay. The section also allows regulations to be made that will enable a reduction in maternity allowance, maternity pay or adoption pay periods to be revoked or to be treated as revoked subject to prescribed conditions and restrictions (for example, the regulation making power might be used in some circumstances where a woman's partner has died).

610. *Subsection (3)* inserts a provision into section 35 to ensure that a woman is not entitled to maternity allowance for any week that she would have been entitled to statutory maternity pay, had she not reduced the duration of the statutory maternity pay period.

611. *Subsection (5)* inserts provisions into section 171ZE to specify that statutory paternity pay will not be payable in respect of a child for a week where the person has already been paid statutory shared parental pay, or taken shared parental leave, in respect of the child or is due to be paid statutory shared parental pay, or take shared parental leave, in respect of the child for any part of that week.

Other statutory rights

Section 121: Statutory rights to leave and pay of prospective adopters with whom looked after children are placed

612. This section supports the changes being made by Part 1, which will provide swifter placement of looked after children in 'Fostering for Adoption' and 'concurrent planning' placements. It amends sections 75A and 80B of the ERA and sections 171ZB, 171ZE, 171ZJ 171ZL, 171ZN and 171ZS of the SSCBA, so that rights to adoption leave and pay and paternity leave and pay can apply to approved adopters who have looked after children placed with them as part of the 'Fostering for Adoption' or 'concurrent planning' processes under section 22C of the Children Act 1989.

613. *Subsection (1)* inserts a new provision into section 75A of the ERA which sets out conditions that may be prescribed for entitlement to ordinary adoption leave in cases relating to placement under section 22C of the Children Act 1989. These conditions are that the person must be a local authority foster parent, must be approved as a prospective adopter and must have been notified by a local authority in England that a child is to be, or is expected to be, placed with the employee under section 22C.

614. *Subsection (2)* inserts new provisions into section 80B of the ERA relating to entitlement to paternity leave. These new provisions enable regulations that are made under section 80(1) of the ERA to be revised so that paternity leave is available for the employed partners of adopters who have or expect to have a child placed with them under section 22C of the Children Act 1989. They also enable those regulations to make provision ensuring that the employee has no entitlement to take a subsequent period of paternity leave in respect of a child if they have already exercised their right to take paternity leave.

615. *Subsection (3)* inserts new subsections (8) and (9) into section 171ZB of the SSCBA, relating to entitlement to statutory paternity pay. New subsection (8) provides that the reference in subsection (2) to a child being placed for adoption is to be treated, where relevant, as including placement under section 22C of the Children Act 1989. This allows regulations setting out conditions of entitlement to paternity pay to include cases where children are placed with prospective adopters under section 22C of the Children Act 1989. Subsection (3) also makes related necessary changes to other references in subsections (3), (6) and (7) of section 171ZE of the SSCBA. New subsection (9) has the effect that a person has no further entitlement to statutory paternity pay in respect of the placement of a child for adoption if he or she has already become entitled to statutory paternity pay in respect of that child in connection with the placement of the child under section 22C.

616. *Subsection (4)* inserts a new subsection (12) into section 171ZE of the SSCBA relating to the rate and period of statutory paternity pay, so that references in section 171(3)(b) and (10) to being placed for adoption should be read, in relevant cases, as being references to being placed under section 22C of the Children Act 1989.

617. *Subsection (5)* inserts new subsections (9) and (10) into section 171ZL of the SSCBA (entitlement to statutory adoption pay). These have the effect that various references to placement for adoption in section 171ZL shall be treated in relevant cases as referring to the placement of a child under section 22C of the Children Act 1989. They also have the effect that a person who has become entitled to statutory adoption pay in respect of a child who is (or is expected to be) placed under section 22C will not be entitled to a further period of statutory adoption pay if he or she is subsequently notified that child will (or is expected to) be placed with him or her for adoption.

Section 122: Statutory rights to leave and pay of applicants for parental orders

618. This section makes provision for intended parents in surrogacy arrangements, who are or will be entitled and intend to make an application for a parental order under section 54

of the Human Fertilisation and Embryology Act 2008, to be entitled to paternity leave and pay and to adoption leave and pay in respect of the child who is or will be the subject of the order.

619. *Subsection (1)* amends section 75A of the ERA to enable the Secretary of State by regulation to apply the provisions for ordinary adoption leave to cases involving an employee who has applied or intends to apply, with another person, for a parental order under section 54 of the Human Fertilisation and Embryology Act 2008 in respect of the child who is, or will be, the subject of the parental order.

620. *Subsection (2)* amends section 75B of the ERA to enable the Secretary of State by regulation to apply the provisions for additional adoption leave to the employee and child as described above for ordinary adoption leave.

621. *Subsection (3)* amends section 75D of the ERA to enable the Secretary of State, when making regulations concerning ordinary or additional adoption leave which concern cases involving an application for a parental order, to require the employee to make a statutory declaration as to his or her eligibility, with another person, to apply for a parental order and to state their intention to make such an application.

622. *Subsection (4)* amends section 80B of the ERA to enable the Secretary of State to make regulations to provide that ordinary paternity leave following birth may apply to intended parents in surrogacy cases where an employee, with another person, is eligible and intends to apply for a parental order in respect of the child who is the subject of such an order.

623. *Subsection (5)* amends section 171ZK of the SSCBA concerning ordinary paternity pay so that regulations may apply ordinary paternity pay to qualifying intended parents in surrogacy arrangements.

624. *Subsection (6)* amends Part 12ZB of the SSCBA concerning statutory adoption pay by creating two new subsections. New subsection (2) enables regulations to be made to apply statutory adoption pay to qualifying intended parents in surrogacy arrangements. New subsection (3) enables the regulations in those cases to impose requirements on intended parents in surrogacy arrangements to provide statutory declarations as to their eligibility and intention to apply for a parental order.

Section 123: ***Statutory paternity pay: notice requirement and period of payment***

625. This section amends the existing provisions in the SSCBA on statutory paternity pay.

626. *Subsection (2)* amends section 171ZC so that the requirement to give notice reflects the changes to the period of payment of statutory paternity pay made by *subsection (3)*. The amendments of section 171ZC also provide a power for the Secretary of State to set the amount of notice which the person must give. *Subsection (3)* amends section 171ZE to give the Secretary of State power to set the number of weeks of statutory paternity pay in regulations subject to a minimum of 2 weeks. It also allows regulations to be made to enable paternity pay to be taken in non-consecutive periods of not less than one week.

627. *Subsection (4)* requires that regulations which set the number of weeks of statutory paternity pay will be subject to the affirmative parliamentary procedure.

Section 124: ***Rate of statutory adoption pay***

628. *Subsection (1)* repeals subsection (1) of section 171ZN of the SSCBA, and provides for the rate of statutory adoption pay to be paid at an earnings related rate for the first 6 weeks and the lower of an earnings related rate or a prescribed weekly rate, whichever is the lower, for the remaining weeks of statutory adoption pay.

629. It also sets the earnings related rate to be the equivalent of 90 per cent of a person's normal weekly earnings for the 8 weeks ending the week in which the person was

notified of the adoption match. The prescribed weekly rate must not be lower than the highest weekly rate that has been set for statutory sick pay.

630. *Subsection (2)* repeals the entry in section 176(1)(a) of the SSCBA which relates to section 171ZN(1) of that Act (as section 171ZN(1) is repealed by *subsection (1)*).

Section 125: Abolition of additional paternity leave and additional statutory paternity pay

631. This section removes the statutory rights to additional paternity leave and additional statutory paternity pay.

632. *Subsection (1)* repeals the additional paternity leave provisions, for birth parents and adopters, from the ERA.

633. *Subsection (2)* repeals the additional statutory paternity pay provisions, for both birth parents and adopters, from Part 12ZA of the SSCBA.

Section 126: Further amendments

634. This section gives effect to Schedule 7. It also shows how references to "ordinary statutory paternity pay" and "statutory paternity pay" in instruments, documents and enactments are to be read once the Act renames "ordinary statutory paternity pay" as "statutory paternity pay" (which is the name this form of statutory pay had before it was changed by the Work and Families Act 2006).

Schedule 7: Statutory rights to leave and pay: further amendments

635. Schedule 7 makes consequential amendments to a number of Acts in light of the introduction of shared parental leave and pay.

636. Many of the paragraphs make amendments to other legislation to re-name "ordinary statutory paternity pay" and "ordinary paternity leave" as "statutory paternity pay" and "paternity leave". With the abolition of additional statutory paternity pay and leave there will only be one type of paternity leave and pay and the references to "ordinary" are no longer necessary.

637. Secondly, the amendments remove references to "additional paternity leave" and "additional paternity pay" where appropriate, in line with the abolition of additional statutory paternity pay and leave.

638. Thirdly, the amendments insert references to "statutory shared parental pay" and "shared parental leave" where appropriate.

639. *Paragraphs 1 to 4* amend Schedule 5 to the Social Security Act 1989. *Paragraphs 2 and 3* amend the existing paragraphs of Schedule 5 about employment-related schemes that contain unfair paternity leave provisions and unfair adoption leave provisions so that they also apply in cases relating to placement of a child under section 22C of the Children Act 1989 (Fostering for Adoption cases) and in cases involving surrogacy arrangements. *Paragraph 4* adds a new paragraph to Schedule 5 about employment-related schemes that contain unfair shared parental leave provisions.

640. *Paragraph 5* amends section 182 of the Finance Act 1989 (which concerns offences relating to the disclosure of information relating to social security functions). One of the ways in which it is amended is so that social security functions include functions relating to statutory shared parental pay.

641. *Paragraph 34(3) and (5)* amend powers in the ERA to allow the Secretary of State to set out in secondary legislation the nature of the right to return to work following a period of paternity leave which was combined with a period of shared parental leave.

642. *Paragraph 48* provides for provisions in the Finance Act 1999 about electronic communication to apply to additional statutory paternity pay.

Part 8 – Time Off Work: Ante-Natal Care Etc

Section 127: Time off work to accompany to ante-natal appointments

643. *Subsection (1)* inserts new sections 57ZE to 57ZI in the Employment Rights Act 1996 (ERA) and *subsection (2)* amends sections 47C, 99 and 225 of the ERA.

644. New section 57ZE creates a right for an employee to take time off during working hours to accompany a pregnant woman to an ante-natal appointment made on the advice of a designated health care professional. The right is available to:

- The husband, civil partner or partner of the pregnant woman;
- The father or parent of the pregnant woman's expected child; and
- An intended parent in a surrogacy situation who meets specified conditions.

645. The right to take time off under section 57ZE can be exercised on up to two occasions for a maximum of six and a half hours on each occasion. An employee is not entitled to take time off unless the employee gives the employer (if the employer so requests) a declaration in the specified form.

646. New section 57ZF provides that an employee who is unreasonably refused time off by an employer may present a complaint to an employment tribunal within the designated time limits. If the complaint is substantiated, the tribunal must make an order to this effect and must award compensation of twice the hourly salary of the employee for the period of absence.

647. New section 57ZG creates a right for certain agency workers to take time off during working hours to accompany a pregnant woman to an ante-natal appointment made on the advice of a designated health care professional. The right is available to:

- The husband, civil partner or partner of the pregnant woman;
- The father or parent of the pregnant woman's expected child; and
- An intended parent in a surrogacy situation who meets specified conditions.

648. The right to take time off under section 57ZG can be exercised on up to two occasions for a maximum of six and a half hours on each occasion. An agency worker is not entitled to take time off unless the agency worker gives the temporary work agency or hirer (if either of them so request) a declaration in the specified form.

649. New section 57ZH provides that an agency worker unreasonably refused time off by the temporary work agency, the hirer, or both, may present a complaint to an employment tribunal within the designated time limits. If the complaint is substantiated, the tribunal must make an order to this effect and must award compensation of twice the hourly salary of the agency worker for the period of absence. Where both the temporary work agency and hirer have unreasonably refused time off, the tribunal can apportion the compensation according to each party's relative fault.

650. New section 57ZI sets out which agency workers have the right to time off under section 57ZG.

651. *Subsection (2)(a)* and *(b)* amend sections 47C and 99 of the ERA to give an employee a right not to be subjected to a detriment and a right not to be unfairly dismissed, as a result of exercising or proposing to exercise a right to time off work to accompany a pregnant woman to an ante-natal appointment. A similar right for an agency worker not to be subjected to a detriment is created in section 129.

652. *Subsection (2)(c)* amends section 225 of the ERA to provide that the calculation date to be used for determining a week's pay for an employee is the date of the appointment in question.

Section 128: Time off work to attend adoption appointments

653. This section inserts new sections 57ZJ to 57ZS into Part VI of the ERA, and makes provision for employed single adopters, or employed adoptive couples, to take time off to attend appointments relating to the placement of a child for adoption or for "Fostering for Adoption" (as to which, see the commentary on section 2). The purpose of the appointments is to enable the adopter(s) to bond with the child and to meet with professionals involved in the care of the child, thus increasing the chances of the adoption being successful.

Section 57ZJ: Right to paid time off to attend adoption appointments

654. Section 57ZJ creates a new right for employees to take paid time off work to attend adoption appointments.

655. Subsection (1) creates a right for an employed single adopter who has been notified by an adoption agency that a child is to be, or is expected to be, placed for adoption with him or her, to take time off to attend an appointment for the purpose of having contact with the child or for any other purpose connected with the adoption (an "adoption appointment").

656. Subsection (2) creates a right for an employee who has been notified by an adoption agency that a child is to be, or is expected to be, placed for adoption with the employee and another person jointly, to take time off to attend an adoption appointment, provided they have elected to exercise the right to take time off under this subsection.

657. Subsection (3) provides that the employee cannot elect to take time off under subsection (2) if they have already elected to take time off under section 57ZL(1)(b) (unpaid time off), or if the other joint adopter, being an employee or an agency worker, has already elected to take time off under subsection (2)(b) or section 57ZN(2)(b).

658. Subsection (4) provides that an employee is not entitled to take time off to attend adoption appointments under section 57ZJ on or after the date of the child's placement for adoption with the employee.

659. Subsection (5) limits the number of adoption appointments that may be taken under section 57ZJ to no more than five for any particular adoption.

660. Subsection (6) limits the maximum amount of time off for each adoption appointment to six and a half hours.

661. Subsection (7) provides that the adoption appointment must have been arranged by or at the request of the adoption agency which made the notification of the placement or the expected placement for adoption.

662. Subsection (8) provides a single adopter is not entitled to take time off under subsection (1) unless he or she provides their employer upon request with a document showing the date and time of the adoption appointment in question and that it has been arranged by an adoption agency.

663. Subsection (9) provides that a joint adopter employee is not entitled to take time off under subsection (2), unless the employee provides their employer upon request with a document that shows the date and time of the adoption appointment and a signed declaration stating that they have made an election to take time off under subsection (2)(b).

664. Subsection (10) provides that the document that shows the date and time of the appointment or the declaration relating to the election under subsection (8) or (9) can be in electronic form.

665. Subsection (11) makes provision to modify the operation of section 57ZJ where more than one child is to be, or is expected to be, placed as part of the same arrangement (for example, where siblings are to be placed with the same adopter) so that, where the adoption appointments relate to the adoption of more than one child: the election under subsection (2)(b) relates to all the children, the maximum number of adoption appointments remains five in total, and the date after which no time off can be taken to attend an adoption appointment is the placement date of the first child.

666. Subsection (12) provides that the working hours of an employee are to be taken to be any time in accordance with the employee's contract of employment that they are required to be at work.

667. Subsection (13) provides that in section 57ZJ "adoption agency" has the meaning given in section 2 of the Adoption and Children Act 2002 or as defined in section 119(1)(a) of the Adoption and Children (Scotland) Act 2007.

Section 57ZK: Right to remuneration for time off for adoption appointments

668. Subsection (1) makes provision for an employee entitled to attend adoption appointments under section 57ZJ to be paid remuneration by his or her employer for the number of working hours for which the employee is entitled to be absent at the appropriate hourly rate.

669. Subsection (2) makes provision that the hourly rate will be the amount of one week's pay divided by the number of normal working hours in a week for that employee when employed under the contract of employment in force on the day when the time off is taken.

670. Subsection (3) makes provision that where the number of normal working hours differs from week to week or over a longer period, the amount of one week's pay shall be divided instead by the average number of normal working hours calculated by dividing by twelve the total number of the employee's normal working hours during the period of twelve weeks ending with the last complete week before the day on which the time off is taken. Or, where an employee has not been employed for a sufficient period to enable the calculation based on twelve weeks to be made, a number is used which fairly represents the number of normal working hours in a week, having regard to specified considerations.

671. Subsection (4) stipulates the specific considerations required to be borne in mind by section 57ZK(3) when choosing a number of weeks to divide the employee's salary by when the employee has not been employed for twelve weeks.

672. Subsection (5) provides that any amount of remuneration for time off under subsection (1) does not affect any right to contractual remuneration. However, subsections (6) and (7) provide that any contractual remuneration paid by an employer for time off under section 57ZJ will go towards discharging any liability of that employer to pay remuneration under section (1), and vice versa.

Section 57ZL: Right to unpaid time off to attend adoption appointments

673. Subsection (1) creates a right for an employed adopter who has been notified by an adoption agency that a child is to be, or is expected to be, placed for adoption with him or her and another person jointly, to take time off to attend an appointment for the purpose of having contact with the child or for any other purpose connected with the adoption (an "adoption appointment"), provided he or she has elected to take time off under subsection (1)(b).

674. Subsection (2) provides that an employee may not elect to take time off under subsection (1) if they have already elected to take paid time off under section 57ZJ, or if the other joint adopter has already elected to take unpaid time off under subsection (1)(b) or under section 57ZP(1)(b).

675. Subsection (3) provides that an employee is not entitled to take time off to attend adoption appointments under section 57ZJ on or after the date of the child's placement for adoption with the employee.

676. Subsections (4) and (5) limit the number of adoption appointments that may be taken under section 57ZL to two appointments of six and a half hours each.

677. Subsection (6) provides that the adoption appointment must have been arranged by or at the request of the adoption agency which made the notification of the placement or the expected placement for adoption.

678. Subsection (7) provides that an employee is not entitled to take time off under this section unless he or she provides their employer upon request with a document showing the date and time of the adoption appointment in question and that it has been arranged by an adoption agency, and a signed declaration that he or she has made an election for the purposes of subsection (1)(b). The declaration or document may be in electronic form (subsection (8)).

679. Subsection (9) makes provision to modify the operation of section 57ZL where more than one child is to be, or is expected to be, placed as part of the same arrangement (for example, where siblings are to be placed with the same adopter) so that, where the adoption appointments relate to the adoption of more than one child: the election under subsection (1)(b) relates to all the children, the maximum number of adoption appointments remains two in total and the date after which no time off can be taken to attend an adoption appointment is the placement date of the first child.

680. Subsection (10) provides that the working hours of an employee are to be taken to be any time in accordance with the employee's contract of employment that they are required to be at work.

681. Subsection (11) provides that in section 57ZJ "adoption agency" has the meaning given in section 2 of the Adoption and Children Act 2002 or as defined in section 119(1)(a) of the Adoption and Children (Scotland) Act 2007.

Section 57ZM: Complaint to employment tribunal

682. This section provides that an employee who is unreasonably refused time off under section 57ZJ or 57ZL to attend an adoption appointment by an employer, or is not paid amounts due under section 57ZK may present a complaint to an employment tribunal within the designated time limits. If the complaint is substantiated, the tribunal must make an order to this effect. The tribunal must also, where the complaint is that time off was refused, award compensation of twice the hourly rate multiplied by the number of hours absence the employee would have been entitled to had it not been refused. If the complaint is that amounts due under section 57ZK are unpaid, the tribunal must also order payment of the unpaid amount.

Section 57ZN: Right to paid time off to attend adoption appointments: agency workers

683. Section 57ZN makes provision for agency workers to take paid time off to attend adoption appointments that is equivalent to that for employees in section 57ZJ. Subsection (12) provides that for the purposes of this section, an agency worker's working hours are any time when the agency worker is required to be at work in accordance with the terms under which the agency worker is working (temporarily) for the hirer.

Section 57ZO: Right to remuneration for time off to attend adoption appointments: agency workers

684. Section 57ZO makes provision for agency workers who are permitted to take time off under section 57ZN that is equivalent to that for employees under section 57ZK. Subsection (1) provides that the temporary work agency must pay remuneration at the appropriate hourly rate for the hours for which the agency worker is entitled to be absent. Subsection (2) sets out how the hourly rate should be calculated in general, but subsection (3) sets out how the calculation should be made in situations where the number of an agency worker's normal working hours differs from week to week.

Section 57ZP: Right to unpaid time off to attend adoption appointments: agency workers

685. Section 57ZP makes provision for agency workers to take unpaid time off to attend adoption appointments that is equivalent to the right for employees to take unpaid time off under section 57ZL. Subsection (10) provides that for the purposes of this section the working hours of an agency worker are any time when he or she is required to be at work (temporarily) for the hirer.

Section 57ZQ: Complaint to employment tribunal: agency workers

686. This section makes provision for agency workers to make complaints to tribunals in respect of refusal of permission to take time off (under section 57ZN or 57ZP) or failure to pay sums due (under section 57ZO) that is equivalent to the provision made for employees under section 57ZM.

Section 57ZR: Agency workers: supplementary

687. This section provides (subsection (1)) that the rights to paid and unpaid time off, and the right to present a complaint to a tribunal, do not apply if the agency worker has not completed the qualifying period, or if there is a break between assignments which means that he or she is no longer entitled to the rights conferred by regulation 5 of the Agency Workers Regulations 2010. Subsection (2) makes clear that the rights to paid and unpaid time off do not impose any duty on the hirer or agency which extends beyond the original intended duration of the assignment. Subsection (3) makes clear that if a person is entitled to take paid or unpaid time off as an employee, then they are excluded from taking paid time or unpaid time off as an agency worker.

Section 129: Right not to be subjected to detriment: agency workers

688. *Subsection (1)* amends section 47C of the ERA to give agency workers a right not to be subjected to a detriment by the temporary work agency or hirer on certain grounds. The grounds are that the agency worker:

- Took or sought to take time off for an ante-natal appointment under section 57ZA or 57ZG of the ERA;
- Received or sought to receive remuneration under section 57ZB of the ERA for time off to attend an ante-natal appointment (only available to pregnant women);
- Took or sought to take time off for an adoption appointment under section 57ZN or 57ZP of the ERA; or
- Received or sought to receive remuneration under section 57ZO of the ERA for time off to attend an adoption appointment (only available to the primary adopter).

689. *Subsection (2)* amends section 48 of the ERA to allow an agency worker who has been subjected to such a detriment to present a complaint to an employment tribunal. It is for the temporary work agency or the hirer to show the ground on which any act or deliberate failure to act was done.

690. *Subsection (3)* amends section 49 of the ERA to provide that if such a complaint is well-founded, the tribunal shall make a declaration to that effect and may award compensation to be paid to the agency worker by the temporary work agency, the hirer, or both.

Section 130: Time off work for ante-natal care: increased amount of award

691. *Subsection (1)* amends section 57 of the ERA to increase the amount of compensation that must be ordered by an employment tribunal which finds that a pregnant employee has unreasonably been refused time off work under section 55 of the ERA to attend an ante-natal appointment. The amount is increased from the hourly salary of the employee for the period of absence to twice that amount.

692. *Subsection (2)* amends section 57ZC of the ERA to increase the amount of compensation that must be ordered by an employment tribunal which finds that a pregnant agency worker has unreasonably been refused time off work under section 57ZA of the ERA to attend an ante-natal appointment. The amount is increased from the hourly salary of the agency worker for the period of absence to twice that amount.

Part 9 – Right to Request Flexible Working

Section 131: Removal of the requirement to be a carer

693. This section removes the requirement that an employee must have parental or caring responsibility in order to make a request to their employer to change their terms and conditions with respect to hours and location of work.

694. *Subsection (1)* repeals section 80F(1)(b) of the ERA which requires an employee to be responsible for the care of a child or in certain cases a person over the age of 18 in order to make a request for flexible working. This means that all employees who have the necessary period of service with their employer (currently 26 weeks) will have a right to request flexible working.

695. *Subsection (2)* also repeals other provisions which are no longer necessary following the removal of the requirement to be the carer of a child or adult.

Section 132: Dealing with applications

696. This section deals with changes to the procedure which employers must follow when dealing with a flexible working request.

697. *Subsection (2)* amends section 80G of the ERA to remove the requirement on employers to follow a statutory procedure when considering flexible working requests. This procedure is currently set out in the Flexible Working (Procedural Requirements) Regulations 2002 (S.I. 2002/3207). These regulations will be revoked. In place of this, *subsection (2)* introduces a duty on employers to consider requests in a reasonable manner.

698. *Subsection (2)* also amends section 80G to introduce a requirement on the employer to notify the employee of its decision within a certain period of time. *Subsection (3)* provides that the employer must give its decision within 3 months beginning on the date that the application is made. This period can be extended by agreement between the employer and employee.

699. *Subsection (4)* sets out the circumstances in which the employer can treat a flexible working request as withdrawn. They are where an employee fails to attend two consecutive meetings to discuss the request or an appeal with their employer without good reason.

Section 133: Complaints to employment tribunals

700. This section amends the rules which apply to the making of a complaint relating to a request for flexible working to an employment tribunal.

701. *Subsection (2)* amends section 80H of the ERA to provide that an employee may make a complaint to an employment tribunal if the employer sought to treat the employee's flexible working request as withdrawn without having grounds to do so. *Subsection (5)* provides that an employee may make this complaint as soon as the employer has informed the employee that it is treating the request as withdrawn.

702. *Subsection (3)* amends section 80H of the ERA to provide a change consequential on the addition of a new ground of complaint.

703. *Subsection (4)* amends section 80H of the ERA to set out the rules on when an employee may make a complaint relating to a flexible working request to an employment tribunal. It provides that an employee cannot make a complaint to an employment tribunal until a final decision has been made by their employer. An employee is required to have exhausted any appeal which is offered by the employer before making a complaint.

704. It also amends section 80H of the ERA to provide that if the employer does not inform the employee of its decision within the required period of time, the employee may make a complaint to an employment tribunal or, if the employer and employee have agreed an extension of time, the employee may make a complaint at the end of the extended period.

705. An employee has a period of three months from the "relevant date" to make a complaint relating to a flexible working request to an employment tribunal. *Subsection (6)* provides that the "relevant date" will be the date on which the employer informed the employee of its final decision. Or, if the employee is complaining that the employer did not have grounds to treat the request as withdrawn, the "relevant date" will be the date on which the employer informs the employee that it is treating the application as withdrawn.

Section 134: Review of sections 131 to 133

706. This section sets out the requirement for the Secretary of State to review sections 131 to 133 of the Act and to set out the conclusions in a report which he or she must publish.

707. The report must include the objectives of the amendments to the ERA; to what extent those objectives have been achieved; and whether the objectives should remain the same and whether there is a less regulatory approach that could achieve the same objectives.

708. The report must be published within 7 years of the sections coming into force and subsequent reports must be published in not more than 7 year intervals from publication of the previous report.

Part 10 – General Provisions

Section 135: Orders and regulations

709. This section provides that all orders and regulations made by the Secretary of State or the Lord Chancellor under the Act are to be made by statutory instrument. Orders made under section 78(6) (*Order relating to the coming into force of the SEN Code of Practice)),* section 137 (*Transitional, transitory or saving provision)* and section 139 *(Commencement)* are not subject to any parliamentary procedure. The first regulations to be made under section 49, an order under section 58(1) or 59(1), regulations under sections 70(3), 92, 93, 94(6), (8), (9) or (10), or under section 94(11) or 136 that amend primary legislation, will be subject to the affirmative resolution procedure. In addition any order made under section 3A of the Adoption and Children Act 2002 (inserted by section 4 of this Act), and the first regulations made under section 4A (inserted by

section 5), and section 128A(4) (inserted by section 7) of that Act are subject to the affirmative resolution procedure. All other orders and regulations made under this Act are subject to the negative resolution procedure.

710. This section allows for orders or regulations to make different provision for different purposes (including different areas) and to make provision generally or in relation to specific cases. Other than in relation to orders made under section 78(6) (*Order relating to the coming into force of the SEN Code of Practice*), section 137 (*Transitional, transitory or saving provision*) or section 139 (*Commencement*), a power to make an order or regulations includes power to make incidental, supplementary, consequential, transitional or transitory provision or saving.

Section 136: ***Consequential amendments, repeals and revocations***

711. This section allows the Secretary of State or the Lord Chancellor to make orders that make consequential amendments to other legislation. By virtue of section 135(6), where such orders amend primary legislation, they will be subject to the affirmative procedure.

Section 137: ***Transitional, transitory or saving provision***

712. *Subsection (1)* allows the Secretary of State or Lord Chancellor to make transitional provision in connection with the commencement of the provisions of the Act.

713. *Subsections (2)* to *(5)* relate to offences contained in the Act which are punishable by the magistrates' court on summary conviction with a fine of £5000. These subsections contain transitional provisions to cater for the situation where section 85 of the Legal Aid, Sentencing and Punishment of Offenders Act 2012 ("the 2012 Act") comes into force on or before the day on which this Act receives Royal Assent.

714. Once section 85 of the 2012 Act is commenced, offences which are punishable by the magistrates' court on summary conviction with a fine of £5000, will be punishable by an unlimited fine instead. In addition, following the commencement of section 85, powers to create an offence punishable by a fine of £5000 will, instead, be able to be exercised to create an offence punishable by a fine of any amount.

715. *Subsection (3)* operates so as to treat the offences listed within that subsection as offences in respect of which section 85(1) of the 2012 Act removes the maximum fine.

716. *Subsection (4)* applies to the power in the new section 69A(1)(b) to be inserted into the Childcare Act 2006 which allows regulations to create offences relating to things done whilst registration with a childminder agency is suspended. *Subsection (4)* operates so as allow an offence to be created by regulations made under new section 69A(1)(b) which is punishable by a fine of any amount.

717. *Subsection (5)* refers to regulations made under section 85 and to regulations made under section 149 of the 2012 Act (Power to make consequential and supplementary provision etc.) which make provision in relation to section 85. *Subsection (5)* allows such regulations to amend, repeal or otherwise modify a provision of this Act or the Childcare Act 2006.

Section 139: ***Commencement***

718. This section provides for the commencement of the Act. The provisions that relate to family justice and that are mentioned in *subsection (3)* will come into force on a date appointed by the Lord Chancellor. Sections 18 (*Repeal of uncommenced provisions of Part 2 of the Family Law Act 1996*), 90 *(extension of licensing of child performances to children under 14)*, 101 *(Local authority functions etc)*, and 102 to 104 *(concerning children's homes)* come into force two months after the date on which the Act is passed. Part 6 comes into force on 1 April 2014. Part 10 (*General Provisions*) comes into force on the date on which the Act is passed. The other provisions of the Act will come into force on a day appointed by the Secretary of State by order, except for section 1 over

which the Welsh Ministers have commencement powers in relation to Wales. Any order made under this section can appoint different days for different purposes.

Section 140: Short title and extent

719. Section 126(2) to (4)*(statutory rights to leave and pay: further amendments)* and section 134 *(review of sections on the right to request flexible working)* extend to England, Wales and Scotland. In some cases section 126(3) and (4) also extends to Northern Ireland. Section 94 extends to the whole of the United Kingdom. Part 10 *(General Provisions)* extends to the whole of the United Kingdom. Save for the repeal made by section 90, where a provision of the Act amends or repeals other legislation, that amendment or repeal has the same extent as the provision which is amended or repealed. Subject to the above the Act extends to England and Wales only.

HANSARD REFERENCES

720. The following table sets out the dates and Hansard references for each stage of the Act's passage through Parliament.

Stage	***Date***	***Hansard reference***
House of Commons		
Introduction	4 February 2013	Vol. 558, col. 48
Second Reading	25 February 2013	Vol. 559, col. 45-134
Committee	5 March 2013	Public Bill Committee Children and Families Bill
	7 March 2013	
	12 March 2013	
	14 March 2013	
	19 March 2013	
	21 March 2013	
	15 April 2013	
	16 April 2013	
	18 April 2013	
	23 April 2013	
	25 April 2013	
Report	11 June 2013	Vol. 564, col. 175-285
Third Reading	11 June 2013	Vol. 564, co.l 285-294
Commons Consideration of Lords Amendments	10 February 2014	Vol. 575, col. 600-666
Royal Assent	14 March 2014	Vol. 577, col. 455
House of Lords		
Introduction	12 June 2013	Vol. 745, col. 1604
Second Reading	2 July 2013	Vol. 746, col. 1092-1202
Committee	9 October 2013	Vol. 748, col. GC1-GC56
	14 October 2013	Vol. 748, col. GC129-GC194
	16 October 2013	Vol. 748, col. GC227-GC284

These notes refer to the Children and Families Act 2014 (c.6) which received Royal Assent on 13 March 2014

Stage	***Date***	***Hansard reference***
	21 October 2013	Vol. 748, col. GC285-GC334
	23 October 2013	Vol. 748, col. GC359-GC424
	28 October 2013	Vol. 748, col. GC489-GC548
	30 October 2013	Vol. 748, col. GC593-GC654
	4 November 2013	Vol. 749, col. GC1-GC60
	6 November 2013	Vol. 749, col. GC61-GC122
	11 November 2013	Vol. 749, col. GC187-GC250
	18 November 2013	Vol. 749, col. GC295-GC370
	20 November 2013	Vol. 749, col. GC403-GC496
Report	9 December 2013	Vol. 750, col. 590-660
	17 December 2013	Vol. 750, col. 1143-1217
	7 January 2014	Vol. 750, col. 1397-1490
	28 January 2014	Vol. 751, col. 1116-1200
	29 January 2014	Vol. 751, col. 1215-1270 and 1299-1350
Third Reading	5 February 2014	Vol. 752, col. 204-256
Royal Assent	13 March 2014	Vol. 752, col. 1855

ANNEX A – FURTHER DETAIL ON FAMILY JUSTICE PROVISIONS:

WELFARE OF THE CHILD: PARENTAL INVOLVEMENT

721. A process map and examples are set out on the following page in order to further explain how the presumption is expected to fit with the decision making process.

722. Below are five example scenarios included to illustrate how the court might apply the presumption in practice. The purpose of these examples is to explain how the presumption is expected to fit with the decision making process and the result reached by the court in each case would of course depend entirely on the facts of the particular case. These examples are in no way intended to suggest that a particular decision should be reached in a particular case.

723. The following fictitious examples are included in order to illustrate how the court might apply the presumption in practice. The purpose of these examples is to explain how the presumption is expected to fit with the decision making process and the result reached by the court in each case would of course depend entirely on the facts of the particular case. These examples are in no way intended to suggest that a particular decision should be reached in a particular case.

EXAMPLE 1

724. Parent A and Parent B are married and have one child together. Parent A left the marital home and Parent B refuses to let Parent A see their child. Parent A wants to be able to see the child at the weekends. Parent A applies for a child arrangements order that sets out that the child should stay over with Parent A from Saturday evening until Sunday morning.

725. Each parent is treated by the court as being able to have safe involvement with the child as no concerns are raised that Parent A or Parent B pose a risk of harm to the child. The presumption therefore applies in respect of each parent and the court has to presume that it will further the welfare of the child for Parent A and Parent B to be involved in the child's life.

726. Parent B is very hurt and upset that Parent A left the marital home and feels that by leaving the home, Parent A has forsaken any "rights" to the child. Parent B, however, does not allege that it would not further the child's welfare for Parent A to have involvement in the child's life.

727. The court has evidence before it that the child had a very good relationship with Parent A before Parent A left the marital home. The court also has evidence relating to the child's wishes and feelings that the child wants to see and stay with Parent A.

728. The presumption stands in respect of both Parent A and Parent B. The court makes its decision, weighing the presumption alongside the other considerations in section 1 of the Children Act 1989, with the child's welfare remaining at all times the court's paramount consideration.

EXAMPLE 2

729. Parent A and Parent B are married and have one child together. Parent A left the marital home and Parent B refuses to let Parent A see their child. Parent A wants to be able to see the child at the weekends. Parent A applies for a child arrangements order that sets out that the child should stay over with Parent A from Saturday evening until Sunday morning.

730. The court receives a section 7 "welfare report" from the Cafcass officer that Parent B has suffered continual emotional abuse at the hands of Parent A and that such abuse was witnessed by the child and distressed the child. The court decides that it is not able

to decide whether Parent A can be involved in the child's life without causing a risk of harm, without hearing further evidence.

731. The court hears evidence regarding the emotional abuse and the effect that it has on the child. It also hears that the child wants to see Parent A and has a very good relationship with Parent A's mother (Grandmother A) who is on good terms with Parent B. The court decides that Parent A could have involvement in the child's life that does not pose a risk of harm if the child has indirect contact with Parent A or contact with Parent A at Grandmother A's house in a situation where Parent A does not come into contact with Parent B (so Grandmother A could collect the child to take home and Parent A would visit at Grandmother A's house).

732. The presumption therefore applies and the court has to presume that it will further the welfare of the child for Parent A to be involved in the child's life. Parent B is very scared of Parent A as a result of years of emotional abuse. Parent B does not, however, allege that it would be contrary to the child's welfare for Parent A to have any involvement with the child. Parent B would prefer that Parent A has indirect contact only of the nature of occasional letter writing. The court has evidence before it that the child often used to spend time at Grandmother A's house when Parent A used to take the child to visit her and that the involvement by Parent A in the child's life in that context was found enjoyable by and rewarding to the child.

733. The presumption stands in respect of both Parent A and Parent B. The court makes its decision, weighing the presumption alongside the other considerations in section 1 of the Children Act 1989, with the child's welfare remaining at all times the court's paramount consideration.

EXAMPLE 3

734. Parent A and Parent B are married and have one child together. Parent A left the marital home and Parent B refuses to let Parent A see their child. Parent A wants to be able to see the child at the weekends. Parent A applies for a [child arrangements order] that sets out that the child should stay over with Parent A from Saturday evening until Sunday morning.

735. Parent B alleges that Parent A has a history of emotionally and physically abusing Parent B and the child. Parent B alleges that Parent A cannot be involved in any way in the child's life without posing a risk of harm to the child. The section 7 welfare report from Cafcass confirms that this is the case and confirms that Parent A has caused such harm to the child in the past that the child feels extremely distressed at the thought of any contact with Parent A. There is also an allegation before the court that Parent A has sent the child threatening letters which also contain abuse levelled at the child. Parent A disputes this account. The court decides, after a consideration of all the evidence, that the prospect of any contact with Parent A would pose a risk of harm to the child and concludes that it is probable that even indirect contact in the form of letter writing would harm the child. The court therefore decides that the presumption does not apply.

736. Parent A's lawyer argues that Parent A has rights under Article 8 of the ECHR which should mean that some form of contact should be ordered. The court balances the Article 8 rights of Parent A against those of the child and Parent B and follows Strasbourg jurisprudence which holds that when there is a conflict between Article 8 rights, the child's rights prevail.

737. The court makes its decision, weighing the fact that the presumption does not apply to Parent A alongside the other considerations in section 1 of the Children Act 1989, with the child's welfare remaining at all times the court's paramount consideration.

EXAMPLE 4

738. Parent A and Parent B are married and have one child together. Parent A left the marital home and Parent B refuses to let Parent A see their child. Parent A wants to be able to see the child at the weekends. Parent A applies for a child arrangements order that sets out that the child should stay over with Parent A from Saturday evening until Sunday morning.

739. Each parent is treated by the court as being able to have safe involvement with the child as no concerns are raised that Parent A or Parent B pose a risk of harm to the child. The presumption therefore applies and the court has to presume that it will further the welfare of the child for Parent A to be involved in the child's life.

740. The child is 15 years old and the court has before it a section 7 welfare report that sets out that the child does not want to see Parent A or have any contact with Parent A as Parent A finds it difficult to come to terms with a recent declaration from the child that the child is gay and Parent A has refused to acknowledge that the child is gay. The child has expressed a strong wish to be able to explore issues of sexuality and feels that any contact with Parent A would inhibit this. The court decides that at the moment the child's welfare will not be furthered by involvement with Parent A and the presumption is rebutted.

741. The court makes its decision, weighing this factor alongside the other considerations in section 1 of the Children Act 1989, with the child's welfare remaining at all times the court's paramount consideration.

EXAMPLE 5

742. Parent A and Parent B were married and had a child. Their marriage has subsequently broken down, and the child lives with Parent B and has regular contact with Parent A. Parent A applies for a child arrangements order that sets out that the child should live with Parent A full time and alleges that Parent B poses a risk of harm to the child.

743. Parent A claims that Parent B has been verbally and physically abusive to the child on several occasions. The court hears evidence of Parent A's allegations, which are supported by other witnesses.

744. The court is of the view after considering the evidence that Parent B poses a risk of harm to the child. The court considers that despite the risk of harm presented by the current arrangement, so long as Parent B is not left alone with the child, it would be possible for Parent B to continue to have some form of involvement in the child's life that would not expose the child to a risk of harm, such as indirect or supervised contact, accordingly the presumption applies in respect of parent B and the court presumes that the child's welfare would be furthered by such involvement.

745. There is no evidence to suggest that Parent A poses any risk of harm to the child, in fact there is a strong relationship between the child and Parent A. On that basis the presumption stands in respect of Parent A and the court presumes that the child's welfare would be furthered by the involvement of Parent A in the child's life. There is no evidence advanced by Parent B to suggest otherwise.

746. The presumption stands in respect of both Parent B and Parent A. The court makes its decision, weighing the presumption alongside the other considerations in section 1 of the Children Act 1989, with the child's welfare remaining at all times the court's paramount consideration.

ANNEX B: TERRITORIAL EXTENT AND APPLICATION TABLE:

Section Number	Title	Application of Section
	PART 1	
	ADOPTION AND CONTACT	
	Adoption	
1	Contact between prescribed persons and adopted person's relatives	England and Wales only
2	Placement of looked after children with prospective adopters	England only
3	Repeal of requirement to give due consideration to ethnicity: England	England only
4	Recruitment, assessment and approval of prospective adopters	England only
5	Adoption support services: personal budgets	England only
6	Adoption support services: duty to provide information	England only
7	The Adoption and Children Act Register	England, Wales and Scotland
	Contact	
8	Contact: children in care of local authorities	England and Wales only
9	Contact: post-adoption	England and Wales only
	PART 2	
	FAMILY JUSTICE	
10	Family mediation information and assessment meetings	England and Wales only
11	Welfare of the child: parental involvement	England and Wales only
12	Child arrangements orders	England and Wales only
13	Control of expert evidence, and of assessments, in children proceedings	England and Wales only
14	Care, supervision and other family proceedings: time limits and timetables	England and Wales only
15	Care plans	England and Wales only
16	Care proceedings and care plans: regulations: procedural requirements	England and Wales only
17	Repeal of restrictions on divorce and dissolution etc where there are children	England and Wales only
18	Repeal of uncommenced provisions of Part 2 of the Family Law Act 1996	England and Wales only
	PART 3	
	CHILDREN AND YOUNG PEOPLE IN ENGLAND WITH SPECIAL EDUCATIONAL NEEDS OR DISABILITIES	

Section Number	Title	Application of Section
	Local authority functions: general principles	
19	Local authority functions: supporting and involving children and young people	England only
	Special educational needs etc	
20	When a child or young person has special educational needs	England only
21	Special educational provision, health care provision and social care provision	England only
	Identifying children and young people with special educational needs and disabilities	
22	Identifying children and young people with special educational needs and disabilities	England only
23	Duty of health bodies to bring certain children to local authority's attention	England only
	Children and young people for whom a local authority is responsible	
24	When a local authority is responsible for a child or young person	England only
	Education, health and care provision: integration and joint commissioning	
25	Promoting integration	England only
26	Joint commissioning arrangements	England only
	Review of education and care provision	
27	Duty to keep education and care provision under review	England only
	Co-operation and assistance	
28	Co-operating generally: local authority functions	England only
29	Co-operating generally: governing body functions	England only
	Information and advice	
30	Local offer	England only
31	Co-operating in specific cases: local authority functions	England only
32	Advice and information	England only
	Mainstream education	
33	Children and young people with EHC plans	England only
34	Children and young people with special educational needs but no EHC plan	England only
35	Children with SEN in maintained nurseries and mainstream schools	England only
	Assessment	
36	Assessment of education, health and care needs	England only

Section Number	Title	Application of Section
Education, health and care plans		
37	Education, health and care plans	England only
38	Preparation of EHC plans: draft plan	England only
39	Finalising EHC plans: request for particular school or other institution	England only
40	Finalising EHC plans: no request for particular school or other institution	England only
41	Independent special schools and special post-16 institutions: approval	England only
42	Duty to secure special educational provision and health care provision in accordance with EHC Plan	England only
43	Schools and other institutions named in EHC plan: duty to admit	England only
44	Reviews and re-assessments	England only
45	Ceasing to maintain an EHC plan	England only
46	Maintaining an EHC plan after young person's 25th birthday	England only
47	Transfer of EHC plans	England only
48	Release of child or young person for whom EHC plan previously maintained	England only
49	Personal budgets and direct payments	England only
50	Continuation of services under section 17 of the Children Act 1989	England only
Appeals, mediation and dispute resolution		
51	Appeals	England only
52	Right to mediation	England only
53	Mediation: health care issues	England only
54	Mediation: educational and social care issues etc	England only
55	Mediation	England only
56	Mediation: supplementary	England only
57	Resolution of disagreements	England only
58	Appeals and claims by children: pilot schemes	England only
59	Appeals and claims by children: follow-up provision	England only
60	Equality Act 2010: claims against schools by disabled young people	England and Wales only
Special educational provision: functions of local authorities		
61	Special educational provision otherwise than in schools, post-16 institutions etc	England only

Section Number	Title	Application of Section
62	Special educational provision outside England and Wales	England only
53	Fees for special educational provision at non-maintained schools and post-16 institutions	England only
64	Supply of goods and services	England only
65	Access to schools, post-16 institutions and other institutions	England only
Special educational provision: functions of governing bodies and others		
66	Using best endeavours to secure special educational provision	England only
67	SEN co-ordinators	England only
68	Informing parents and young people	England only
69	SEN information report	England only
Detained persons		
70	Application of Part to detained persons	England and Wales only
71	Assessment of post-detention education, health and care needs of detained persons	England only
72	Securing EHC plans for certain detained persons	England only
73	EHC plans for certain detained persons: appeals and mediation	England only
74	Duty to keep EHC plans for detained persons	England only
75	Supply of goods and services: detained persons	England only
Information to improve well-being of children and young people with SEN		
76	Provision and publication of special needs information	England only
Code of practice		
77	Code of practice	England only
78	Making and approval of code	England only
79	Review of resolution of disagreements	England only
Supplementary		
80	Parents and young people lacking capacity	England only
81	Disapplication of Chapter 1 of Part 4 of EA 1996 in relation to children in England	England only
82	Consequential amendments	England only
83	Interpretation of Part 3	England only
PART 4		
CHILDCARE ETC		
84	Childminder agencies	England only

Section Number	Title	Application of Section
85	Inspections at request of providers of childcare to young children	England only
86	Repeal of local authority's duty to assess sufficiency of childcare provision	England only
87	Discharge of authority's duty to secure free early years provision	England only
88	Governing bodies: provision of community facilities	England only
89	Childcare costs scheme: preparatory expenditure	England only
PART 5		
WELFARE OF CHILDREN		
90	Extension of licensing of child performances to children under 14	England and Wales only
91	Purchase of tobacco etc. on behalf of persons under 18	England and Wales only
92	Prohibition of sale of nicotine products to persons under 18	England and Wales only
93	Amendments consequential on section 92	England and Wales only
94	Regulation of retail packaging etc of tobacco products	UK-wide
95	Protection of children's health: offence of smoking in a private vehicle	England and Wales only
96	Young carers	England only
97	Parent carers	England only
98	Arrangement for living with former foster parents after reaching adulthood	England only
99	Promotion of educational achievement of children looked after by local authorities	England only
100	Duty to support pupils with medical conditions	England only
101	Local authority functions relating to children etc: intervention	England and Wales only
102	Application of suspension etc powers to establishments and agencies in England	England only
103	Objectives and standards for establishments and agencies in England	England only
104	National minimum standards for establishments and agencies in England	England only
105	Disqualification from carrying on, or being employed in, a children's home	England only
106	Provision of free school lunches	England only
PART 6		

Section Number	**Title**	**Application of Section**
THE CHILDREN'S COMMISSIONER		
107	Primary function of the Children's Commissioner	England primarily. Applies to Scotland, Wales and Northern Ireland where the Children's Commissioner's role in promoting and protecting the rights of children is in relation to non-devolved matters.
108	Provision by Commissioner of advice and assistance to certain children	England primarily. Applies to Scotland, Wales and Northern Ireland where the Children's Commissioner's role in promoting and protecting the rights of children is in relation to non-devolved matters.
109	Commissioner's powers to enter premises	England primarily. Applies to Scotland, Wales and Northern Ireland where the Children's Commissioner's role in promoting and protecting the rights of children is in relation to non-devolved matters.
110	Provision of information to Commissioner	England primarily. Applies to Scotland, Wales and Northern Ireland where the Children's Commissioner's role in promoting and protecting the rights of children is in relation to non-devolved matters.
111	Advisory board	England primarily. Applies to Scotland, Wales and Northern Ireland where the Children's Commissioner's role in promoting and protecting the rights of children is in relation to non-devolved matters.
112	Business plans	England primarily. Applies to Scotland, Wales and Northern Ireland where the Children's Commissioner's role in promoting and protecting the rights of children is in relation to non-devolved matters.
113	Annual reports	England primarily. Applies to Scotland, Wales and

Section Number	Title	Application of Section
		Northern Ireland where the Children's Commissioner's role in promoting and protecting the rights of children is in relation to non-devolved matters.
114	Children living away from home or receiving social care	England primarily. Applies to Scotland, Wales and Northern Ireland where the Children's Commissioner's role in promoting and protecting the rights of children is in relation to non-devolved matters.
115	Children's Commissioner: minor and consequential amendments	England primarily. Applies to Scotland, Wales and Northern Ireland where the Children's Commissioner's role in promoting and protecting the rights of children is in relation to non-devolved matters.
116	Repeal of requirement to appoint Children's Rights Director	England primarily. Applies to Scotland, Wales and Northern Ireland where the Children's Commissioner's role in promoting and protecting the rights of children is in relation to non-devolved matters.
PART 7		
STATUTORY RIGHTS TO LEAVE AND PAY		
Shared parental leave		
117	Shared parental leave	England, Wales and Scotland only
118	Exclusion or curtailment of other statutory rights to leave	England, Wales and Scotland only
Statutory shared parental pay		
119	Statutory shared parental pay	England, Wales and Scotland only
120	Exclusion or curtailment of other statutory rights to pay	England, Wales and Scotland only
Other statutory rights		
121	Statutory rights to leave and pay of prospective adopters with whom looked after children are placed	England, Wales and Scotland only

Section Number	Title	Application of Section
122	Statutory rights to leave and pay of applicants for parental orders	England, Wales and Scotland only
123	Statutory paternity pay: notice requirement and period of payment	England, Wales and Scotland only
124	Rate of statutory adoption pay	England, Wales and Scotland only
125	Abolition of additional paternity leave and additional statutory paternity pay	England, Wales and Scotland only
	Further amendments	
126	Further amendments	In part England, Wales and Scotland; in part Northern Ireland
	PART 8	
	TIME OFF WORK: ANTE-NATAL CARE ETC	
127	Time off work to accompany to ante-natal appointments	England, Wales and Scotland only
128	Time off work to attend adoption appointments	England, Wales and Scotland only
129	Right not to be subjected to detriment: agency workers	England, Wales and Scotland only
130	Time off work for ante-natal care: increased amount of award	England, Wales and Scotland only
	PART 9	
	RIGHT TO REQUEST FLEXIBLE WORKING	
131	Removal of requirement to be a carer	England, Wales and Scotland only
132	Dealing with applications	England, Wales and Scotland only
133	Complaints to employment tribunals	England, Wales and Scotland only
134	Review of sections 131 to 133	England, Wales and Scotland only
	PART 10	
	GENERAL PROVISIONS	
135	Orders and regulations	UK-Wide
136	Consequential amendments, repeals and revocations	UK-Wide
137	Transitional, transitory or saving provision	UK-Wide
138	Financial provision	UK-Wide
139	Commencement	UK-Wide
140	Short title and extent	UK-Wide

Adapted and published by GRANGIS under the OGL Licence 3.0.

www.nationalarchives.gov.uk/doc/open-government-licence/version/3/

GRANGIS - UK PUBLISHING 2022.

Thank you for taking the time to leave us a review regarding this version

★★★★★

For further inquiries, contact us at:
www.grangis.com / contact@grangis.com

www.ingramcontent.com/pod-product-compliance
Lightning Source LLC
LaVergne TN
LVHW060213210926
848481LV00008B/2719

* 9 7 9 8 8 8 5 5 9 0 3 5 8 *